pizza

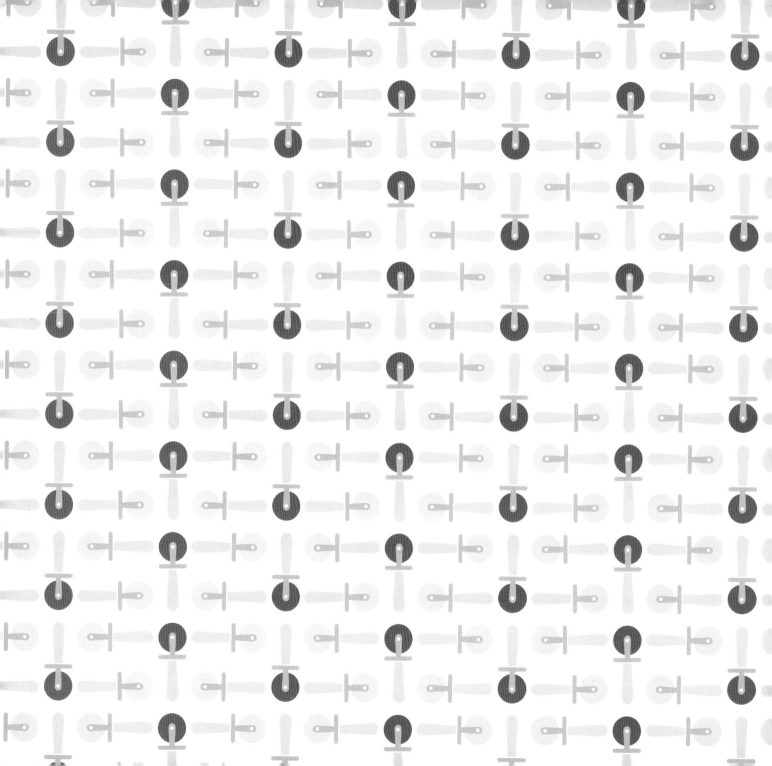

pizza

DIANE MORGAN & TONY GEMIGNANI

Photographs by Scott Peterson

More than 60 recipes for delicious homemade pizza

CHRONICLE BOOKS
SAN FRANCISCO

Library of Congress Cataloging-in-Publication Data available.

ISBN-10: 0-8118-4554-0
ISBN-13: 978-0-8118-4554-0

Manufactured in China.

Design: **Ayako Akazawa**

Typesetting: **Janis Reed**

Prop styling : **Emma Star Jensen**

Food styling: **Andrea Lucich** and **Lorraine Battle**

Photo assistant: **Josh Drescher**

The photographer wishes to thank **Sur La Table** for the generous use of props.

Distributed in Canada by Raincoast Books
9050 Shaughnessy Street
Vancouver, British Columbia V6P 6E5

10 9 8 7 6 5 4 3

Chronicle Books LLC
680 Second Street
San Francisco, California 94107

www.chroniclebooks.com

ACKNOWLEDGMENTS

While working on this book, our ovens were cranked to the highest heat possible, our grills were glowing, and our counters were dusted with flour ready for the next dough to be rolled, stretched, or tossed. For months, sacks of flour, packages of yeast, and refrigerator shelves filled with cheese dominated our kitchens. We wanted to cover pizza in America from its humble roots, starting with a coal-fired brick oven at the back of a grocery store, in New York to the West Coast, where anything goes on top of pizza as long as it tastes great. In the middle of the country, delicious, eat-it-with-a-fork deep-dish pizza has earned its respected place. With the gracious help of colleagues, family, and friends, this pizza book went from a simple concept to a dedicated search for the best pizza recipes and techniques. Without all of you, these insights and recipes wouldn't exist.

DIANE MORGAN THANKS:

My husband, Greg Morgan, love and soul mate for life; and my children, Eric and Molly, my favorite recipe tasters and critics extraordinaire. To Cheryl Russell, my valued and beloved assistant—I don't know what I would do without your support and talent. I offer a very special thank-you to my co-author, Tony Gemignani, whose talent, generosity, and kindness have been a true inspiration. This book wouldn't have been nearly as much fun to work on and write without you.

At Chronicle Books: A huge hug to my terrific editor and dear friend Bill LeBlond; and I am grateful to Amy Treadwell, Michele Fuller, Michael Weisberg, Kendra Kallan, Leslie Jonath, and Jan Hughes for being so wise, creative, and fun, and for all their hard work. Many thanks to Carrie Bradley for her careful line editing.

For so generously giving me great leads, pizza insight and wisdom, and appetites as my pizza tasters, I thank: Marlene Parrish, Sam Selario, Roberto Caporuscio, Cathy Whims, Laura Shapiro, Amy Albert, Tom Boyles, Domenica Marchetti, Laura Werlin, Fred Mortati at Orlando Food Sales, Atimo Caputo at Caputo Flour in Naples, Italy, Belinda Ellis at White Lily Flour, Lynne Devereux at Context Marketing, Lize Willers at Cantare Foods, Jim Freeland at Lou Malnati's, Peter and Harriet Watson, David Watson, Paola Gentry and Eric Watson, Marci and Steve Taylor, Margie and Ken Sanders, Mary and Jack Barber, Sara and Eric Whiteford, Summer Jameson, Josie Jimenez, Roxane and Austin Huang, Ann and Brijesh Anand, Prentice Price, Jennifer Kuhlman, Heidi Yorkshire, Joseph Anthony, Rick Rodgers, Toni Allegra, and Peter Reinhart.

TONY GEMIGNANI THANKS:

My friends, students, competitors, and fellow employees, who have provided so much support, direction, and information over the years. You have broadened my palate and given me the confidence that, in turn, has driven me to be the best I can be. For this I am grateful. Thank you for all the little talks and long walks—memories of you will last a lifetime.

Thank you: Andy Costa of The Pastabilities Are Endless, Andy Lo Russo (The Singing Italian Chef), Big Dave Ostrander (The Pizza Doctor), Sandy Plotkin of Carry Hot/ProdoughUSA (thanks for believing in me), Chef Landry, Brian Cain of Foremost Farms, Ted and Chris Arena of Swiss American Sausage Company, Charlene Rouspil of Dacor Ranges, Dino Ciccone, Don Farlio (thanks for not missing that fishing trip), Emilio Giacametti, Frank Giovanni (thanks for the little talks), George Giove of Brothers Pizza and Big Apple Pizza, the Grande Cheese Company, Bellissimo Foods, Chris Bangs, Todd King and staff of Green Mill restaurants, Jeanie Lauren of Skyanna Entertainment, Michael Dorian and Joe dos Santos of Cat Price Productions, Joe Carlucci, Ken Bryant (my best student and toughest competitor), Marsha Garland, Ann Lukezic, Michael Shepherd, Brian Edler, Pizza Paul Nyland, Pizza Today (my first competition and the one that started it all), Steve and Linda Green, Tom Lehmann (The Dough Doctor), Tom Boyles and all the staff at PMQ, Steve Coomes at pizzamarketplace.com, Joey Altman, Jay Leno and the staff of *The Tonight Show* (my biggest break ever), Jay Sunderwalla, Nick Angileri, Grazziano, Ross Sutherland, Ryan Baldino, Rusty Toth, Siler Chapman, Stanislaus, Supakit Rungrote, and Tom Fuller. In addition, many thanks to culinary director Kathleen Taggart and former director Pamela Keith at Draeger's Cooking School, Karen Alvarez at Andronico's Cooking School, and Doralece Dullaghan at Sur La Table for giving me opportunities to teach.

Contents

Introduction

There are over 61,000 pizzerias in America. Three billion pizzas are eaten every year. More than 11 million tons of pepperoni are consumed each year. It is a $32 billion-a-year industry. From its humble roots as peasant food in Italy, pizza has become the Italian import America has adopted as its own.

From ancient roots as an unleavened wafer spread with oil to the happenstance discovery of leavening by the Egyptians to the travels of the Greeks into southern Italy and the Etruscans who settled in the north, a flat bread was developed by the Neapolitans that has morphed over time into what we now know as pizza. Other styles developed alongside the Neapolitan, such as Roman style, or "pizza by the meter," sold in varying lengths. Once pizza hit the American shores, distinct regional styles developed over time, taking liberties with the traditional toppings and baking techniques. Now we have New York–style pizza, Chicago style, California style, pizzas on the grill, and even dessert pizzas. Not only have pizzerias become a fixture in every city and suburb, now food manufacturers have made it easier to make pizza at home by developing frozen pizza dough, refrigerated pizza dough, and prebaked crusts.

Pizza is an in-depth survey of all of the major styles of pizza making, with a chapter dedicated to each, as well as additional chapters on grilled pizza, quick-and-easy kid-friendly pizzas made with premade crusts, and dessert pizza. Chapter 1 covers all the basics for beginning to make pizza at home. Through recipes and stories, we want to take you on a tour of American pizza. We start from the beginning, focusing on Neapolitan-style pizza in all its authenticity. Diane discovered and studied with a charming, true Neapolitan *pizzaiolo,* Roberto Caporuscio, owner of Roberto's Pizzeria in Pittsburgh, Pennsylvania. Dedicated to the preservation of true Neapolitan pizza, Roberto imports all of his ingredients from Italy, including the flour to make the dough.

Our chapter on Neapolitan pizza reflects those sensibilities and provides the home pizza maker with authentic recipes straight from Roberto. If we thought substituting American all-purpose flour for the Italian flour that Roberto uses—*farina di grano tenero tipo 00*—would yield identical dough, we would have made the substitution; but it's not the same, and we wanted you to have his recipe exactly. His dough is perfection, and now you, too, can make it at home.

New York City is home to the first pizzeria in America. The founding fathers of pizza were Italian immigrants, but the ingredients they found in their new country differed from those they knew in Naples. In New York there was no buffalo's milk mozzarella, so cow's milk mozzarella was used; the tomatoes were different, as was the flour, even the water. Over time, pizza in New York evolved from an individual, 9-inch pie into a large, thin-crust pizza as much as 18 inches in diameter. From a few humble establishments, the number of New York pizzerias has grown to more than three thousand. Our chapter on New York–style pizza gives you some of the stories and legends, and a hearty cross section of beloved regional recipes.

Leave it to the Windy City to turn pizza into a deep-dish wonder. You have to let go of your pizza assumptions in order to successfully make a Chicago-style deep-dish or stuffed pizza at home. Forget the cheese on top—with a deep-dish pizza, the cheese is layered over the dough, then the toppings are added, and the sauce is on top! Unlike thin-crust pies, deep-dish pizzas are no quick trip to the oven—a deep-dish pizza takes at least 30 minutes to bake. Another thing you might find surprising about Chicago-style pizza: The most popular filling isn't meat, it's spinach. Although many may think of Chicago as the home of the hot dog, those deep-dish fans would make Popeye proud.

When most Americans think of California, words like "unconventional," "creative," and "trend-setting" come to mind. That's true for pizza, too. Toppings on the West Coast tend to be exotic, nontraditional—and delicious. Some think it all started with Wolfgang Puck back in the 1970s, when he introduced his signature pizza with smoked salmon, crème fraîche, and caviar. Alice Waters reinterpreted pizza when she opened Chez Panisse and began to make pizzas in a wood-fired oven, using seasonal toppings based on whatever the garden and organic farmers produced. Carrying on in this tradition, Tony has created California-style pizzas for his Bay Area pizzeria, Pyzano's. We've given you Tony's best recipes and his customers' all-time favorite pies. Tony's Famous Cholula Spicy Chicken Pizza (page 93) is not to be missed.

Our chapter on grilling pizza gives you the opportunity to be both a baker and a grillmeister, producing cracker-crisp crusts and smoky, meltingly delectable toppings. Start thinking out of the box as to what tops a pizza, and try our Grilled Pizza with Fig Jam, Prosciutto, Blue Cheese, and Arugula (page 120). Grilled Portobello Mushroom, Green Onion, Pesto, and Fontina Pizza (page 122) delights every vegetarian friend we know.

If the concept of making pizza at home from scratch—starting by working with yeast and waiting for the dough to rise—leaves you thinking, "Well, who has time to do that," visit Chapter 7 for a time-saving approach to homemade pizza. Although we hope you use this book to experience the pleasures of coating your hands with flour and tossing dough, we understand not everyone has the time or the inclination. The recipes in this chapter yield fresh, delicious pizzas using premade crust, with an emphasis on kid-friendliness for busy parents. Assembling the Canadian Bacon, Mozzarella, Pineapple, and Peperoncini

Pizza is a snap (page 129), as is the Very Veggie Pizza with Olives and Artichoke Hearts (page 135). Note that almost every recipe in the book can be made using a prebaked crust, or, for that matter, store-bought refrigerated or frozen pizza dough.

Finally, we just couldn't resist a chapter on dessert pizzas. We've both got a sweet tooth, and Diane readily admits to a chocolate obsession, so making sweet pizzas seemed like a natural. We created a dessert dough, adding honey and spice, and filled a chapter with tempting, delicious toppings. The next time you throw a party, surprise your guests and serve pizza—for dessert!

It's no wonder pizza has been so loved for so long and continues to grow in popularity. If the thought of all these pizzas has made you hungry, then get yourself a pizza stone; fire up your oven as high as it goes; and press, stretch, and toss that dough. You'll be a *pizzaiolo* with your very own neighborhood joint—your home.

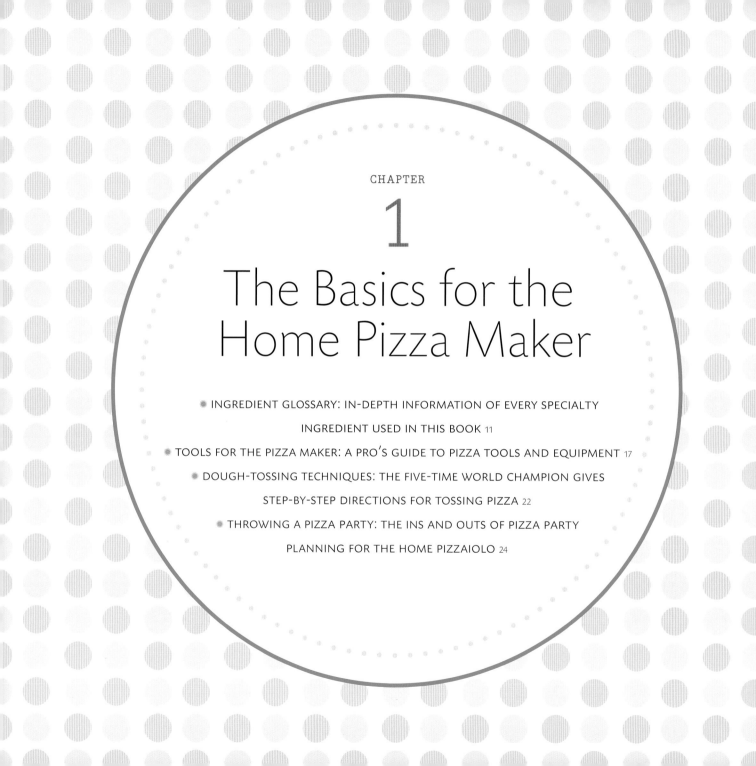

1

The Basics for the Home Pizza Maker

Ingredient Glossary

Here is a glossary of the primary ingredients used throughout this book. Detailed descriptions are given, tips on preparation are discussed, sources for purchasing are mentioned, and some preferences are expressed. Look at our Sources list (page 160) at the back of the book for specialty retailers and online merchants.

CHEESE

BEL PAESE : A semisoft Italian cow's milk cheese, Bel Paese has a mild, buttery flavor. In Italian it means "beautiful country." It is produced south of Milan in Lombardy. Bel Paese is very similar to the French Port Salut. Another good substitute is Italian Gavianella.

BLUE CHEESE OR BLUE-VEINED CHEESES : These aromatic cheeses are marbled with a bluish green mold. They are characteristically salty but can also be buttery, musty, tangy, or even somewhat sweet. There are many fine examples of blue-veined cheeses: English Stilton; Italian Gorgonzola; French Roquefort; Spanish Cabrales; and delicious American blue cheeses such as Maytag Blue, Point Reyes Farmstead Blue, Westfield Farms Hubbardston Blue, and Bingham Hill Blue.

CACIOCAVALLO : Provolone-like in style, the distinctive gourd shape of this Italian cow's milk cheese dates to the days when pairs of Caciocavallo were suspended from a pole to ripen. This is one of the few cheeses produced south of Rome.

FONTINA, ITALIAN : *Fontina Val d'Aosta* is one of the oldest cheeses in Italy. It is made from raw cow's milk and is aged for over 60 days. Fontina has a straw-colored interior with small holes. Its texture is dense, smooth, and slightly elastic, and it has a nutty taste with a hint of honey at the finish. It is a wonderful melting cheese.

GRUYÈRE : This Swiss cow's milk cheese has a rich, nutty, almost sweet flavor. It is made in 100-pound wheels and is aged for 10 to 12 months. It has a golden brown rind and a firm, pale golden interior with medium-sized holes. It is delicious for eating out-of-hand, but is especially suited for cooking. Gruyère is also produced in France, and there is some production of Gruyère in the United States.

MASCARPONE : Often used in desserts, mascarpone is an ivory-colored, buttery-rich cow's milk cream cheese from Italy's Lombardy region. Made either as a double- or triple-cream cheese, mascarpone has a sweet, slightly acidic flavor.

MOZZARELLA : Regular mozzarella, or "pizza cheese," has a semi-soft, elastic texture and is drier and not as delicately flavored as fresh mozzarella. It is a popular cheese for pizza because it has excellent melting qualities. Mozzarella is made with either whole, part-skim, or nonfat milk. For pizza, the mozzarella labeled "low moisture" is the cheese of choice. For the best flavor, we prefer to use whole-milk mozzarella for our pizzas. Buy mozzarella in blocks and grate it yourself. Pre-grated mozzarella sold in plastic packages is coated with either a flour or cornstarch mixture to keep it from sticking together and oxidizing. To our palates it has an unpleasant aftertaste.

MOZZARELLA, FRESH BUFFALO (MOZZARELLA DI BUFALA) : A pulled- or spun-curd cheese made from pasteurized whole buffalo's milk. *Mozzarella di bufala* is porcelain white in color and spherical in shape with a very thin glossy, edible rind. It has a springy texture and a pleasantly sour taste with a faint mossy smell, reminiscent of the humid grazing fields of southern Italy. It comes packed in a whey brine. Two American dairies are now making buffalo mozzarella. See Sources, page 160.

MOZZARELLA, FRESH COW'S MILK (FIOR DI LATTE) : Like *mozzarella di bufala, fior di latte* is a fresh, pulled- or spun-curd cheese made in Italy in the Campania and Apulia regions. Made from pasteurized whole cow's milk, it is moist with a pleasant springy texture and is sweet, milky, and buttery in taste. It is about half the price of *mozzarella di bufala*. There are quite a number of American cheese makers producing delicious fresh cow's milk mozzarella. See Sources, page 160.

PARMESAN : A hard, dry grating cheese made from skimmed or partially skimmed cow's milk, Parmesan has a pale gold rind and a straw-colored interior. It is typically aged for about 14 months. Good Parmesan has a sharp, rich, almost buttery flavor. Parmesan is made in many countries, including the United States; however, nothing compares to Italy's Parmigiano-Reggiano. This cheese can be made only in the provinces of Parma, Reggio Emilia, and Modena in their entirety, and a small portion of two other regions. Laws restrict when this cheese can be made, how it is made, what a wheel must weigh, and how long it must be aged (a minimum of 14 months, although most are aged over 2 years). Look for the words *Parmigiano-Reggiano* stamped on the rind of the cheese to determine its authenticity.

PECORINO ROMANO : Another hard, dry grating cheese, pecorino romano is made from partially skimmed sheep's milk. It has an intense sheep's milk flavor, with peppery overtones and a distinct saltiness. It is used for grating over pasta, combined with vegetables, and sprinkled on pizza, just like Parmesan.

PROVOLONE : This pulled- or spun-curd cow's milk cheese from southern Italy has a firm texture and mild, smoky flavor. It has a golden brown rind and straw-yellow interior. Provolone is formed into melon or torpedo shapes and then bound with rope and hung to dry for proper aging. Most provolone is aged for 2 to 3 months; others, called "sharps," are aged for up to a year, producing a cheese with a more pronounced and smoky flavor.

RICOTTA : A rich, fresh, slightly grainy cheese made with either whole or partially skimmed cow's or sheep's milk, ricotta resembles cottage cheese but is smoother, pure white, and moist with a slightly sweet flavor. Most Italian ricottas (the name means "recooked" in Italian) are made from the whey that is drained off from making mozzarella; in the United States, ricottas are usually made with a combination of whey and milk.

SCAMORZA : A traditional Italian pulled- or spun-curd cow's milk cheese similar to mozzarella. Scamorza has curds with a firmer texture, which, once formed, are allowed to dry. The result is a dense cheese with a salty flavor. It is shaped into braided loaves or small ovals that look like antique money bags, tied with string and hung to ripen for only a brief time, 6 to 15 days. When Scamorza is smoked *(Scamorza affumicata)*, its skin is light brown and it takes on a woodsy, smoked aroma.

CORNMEAL

Cornmeal, available in either white, yellow, or blue versions, is produced by grinding dried kernels. It comes in three grinds: fine, medium, and coarse. We used medium-grind yellow cornmeal for the recipes in this book.

CRÈME FRAÎCHE

Crème fraîche is a cultured cream used in French cooking. Similar to sour cream, crème fraîche is tart and tangy, but a bit thinner and definitely richer. Crème fraîche is now readily available in well-stocked supermarkets, but it is easy to make your own: Combine ½ cup heavy cream (preferably not ultra-pasteurized) and ½ cup sour cream in a jar or small bowl. Stir to thoroughly combine. Cover and let stand in a warm place until thick, 8 to 24 hours. Crème fraîche will keep well for about a week in the refrigerator.

FLOUR

ALL-PURPOSE FLOUR, UNBLEACHED : All-purpose flour is wheat flour blended to contain a moderate amount of protein, usually around 11.5 percent, so it can be used for a wide range of baking. Because unbleached flour has not been treated with a whitening agent, it retains its natural beta-carotene pigments, contributing a subtle flavor to dough.

BREAD FLOUR, UNBLEACHED : Bread flour has a higher protein content than all-purpose flour, 12 to 14 percent. Having a higher protein level gives more structure and elasticity to pizza dough and bread. We tested many types and brands of unbleached (not treated with a whitening agent) bread flour in the course of making pizza dough, and the flour that consistently worked the best was unbleached bread flour with at least 12.5 percent protein. (Although commercial bakers and pizza makers can buy unbleached bread flour that is 13.5 percent protein—this is the kind Tony uses—it isn't readily available at retail.)

CAPUTO FLOUR : *Farina di grano tenero tipo 00,* literally, "flour of soft grain, type 00," is one of only a few Italian 00 flours certified for use in making true Neapolitan pizza by the Association of Real Neapolitan Pizza, a group with 2,500 members worldwide. Thanks to Belinda Ellis at White Lily Flour, a sample of the Caputo brand of this kind of flour was analyzed by their lab. Caputo flour is 100 percent hard wheat with no enrichment. The protein, at 11.5 percent, is lower than most hard-wheat flours. This flour creates a soft, delicate dough very different from other dough recipes. Even using American all-purpose flour with an 11.7 percent protein level did not produce the same results, which is why this flour is being specifically called for in the dough recipe in the chapter on Neapolitan-style pizza. See Sources, page 160, for where to buy Caputo flour.

RYE FLOUR : Milled from a hardy cereal grass, rye flour is dark in color and is lower in protein than either all-purpose or whole-wheat flour. It is usually used in combination with a higher protein flour for baking. Medium rye flour, used in the dough recipe for the grilled pizzas in this book, is the most commonly available rye flour on the market.

MEATS

CHORIZO : Garlic and powdered red chiles dominate the flavor of this Mexican sausage made from highly seasoned, coarsely ground pork. Chorizo is sold either as sausages in casing or in bulk. Look for Mexican chorizo, which is made from fresh pork. Spanish chorizo, though equally delicious, is made from smoked pork and is not the desired type for the recipes in this book.

HAM, ITALIAN : *Prosciutto cotto* and *rosterdet prosciutto di Parma* are specialty baked hams, the latter specifically from Parma. *Prosciutto cotto* is studded and rolled with crushed peppercorns and herbs. *Prosciutto di Parma* is seasoned, salt-cured (but not smoked), and air-dried; it is pressed to give it its characteristic firm, dense texture.

PEPPERONI : A highly seasoned and spicy Italian salami made of pork and beef. It is slender, very firm, and should be sliced paper-thin for pizza. Pepperoni connoisseurs look for those packed in natural casings. Select pepperoni sticks about the size of a quarter in diameter—much smaller than the typical pepperoni sticks—as these will "cup" when baked on top of a pizza.

PORK SAUSAGE, ITALIAN : Italian link sausage is a mixture of fresh ground pork mixed with fat, salt, and other seasonings. You'll usually see mild (sweet) or hot (spicy) sausages sold. Look for sausage made without additives or fillers. Pork sausage is also sold in bulk without casings. Some recipes in this book call for forming sausage into small balls or little chunks to put on top or inside a pizza. Bulk Italian pork sausage comes either mildly spiced (sweet) or seasoned with hot red pepper flakes (spicy).

SALAMI : The *salame* family of sausages comprises those cured without cooking; they are typically air-dried. Genoa salami is the best known of the Italian salamis. It is made from pork and veal and seasoned with pepper, garlic, and red wine. If you can't find Genoa salami, use either *finocchiona* or *soppressata*.

OLIVE OIL

EXTRA-VIRGIN OLIVE OIL : Considered the finest and fruitiest of the olive oils, "extra-virgin" is produced from the first cold-processing of the olives. It can range in color from pale straw to bright green, with the deeper colored oils having the most intense flavor. Products labeled "olive oil" or "pure olive oil" are a blend of refined olive oil and virgin or extra-virgin oil. We use regular olive oil for sautéing and save the expensive extra-virgin olive oil for drizzling on pizza.

ROASTED GARLIC–FLAVORED OLIVE OIL : Supermarkets and specialty stores are giving over more and more shelf space to flavored olive oils, and it's fun to experiment with the different versions available. Roasted garlic olive oil adds a subtle garlic flavor to pizzas. Substitute extra-virgin olive oil if you can't find a garlic-infused oil for recipes that call for it.

SALT

KOSHER SALT : An additive-free coarse rock salt, kosher salt is used by some Jews in the preparation of meat; in addition, for many gourmet cooks, this salt is preferred for its taste and texture. If measured and used in baking, by volume, one needs to use more kosher salt than table salt to achieve the same desired level of saltiness.

SEA SALT : Sea salt is in fact salt recovered through the natural evaporation of seawaters. It comes in either fine-grained or large crystals. By volume, use fine-grained sea salt interchangeably with table salt. Fleur de sel, from Brittany or the Camargue region of France, is one of the most prized sea salts, with large, flaky, grayish crystals and a pure, briny flavor and aroma.

TABLE SALT : The most common salt, table salt is a fine-grained, refined rock salt processed with additives to keep it from caking. (It may or may not have iodine added). Many gourmet cooks prefer to use additive-free salt, either kosher or sea salt, because when tasted side by side, the purity of kosher or sea salt is quite obvious. However, there is no discernable difference in taste when used in baking. By volume, one needs to use less table salt than kosher salt when making dough.

TOMATOES

ROMA : Also called plum or Italian plum tomatoes, the Roma is an ovoid-shaped fruit with a meaty flesh and usually a red skin (there are yellow-skinned varieties, too). In season, they have great flavor; out of season, they tend to be the best-tasting fresh tomato option in the market.

SAN MARZANO : These special tomatoes *(Lycopersicon esculentum)* are a cylindrical, two-lobed fruit from the famed San Marzano region of Italy. This is the tomato preferred for making true Neapolitan pizzas, or for any dish using canned tomatoes. Deep red, firm, and meaty, with very few seeds, they are low in acid and high in fruitiness because they are handpicked when they are fully ripened. Look for cans marked "San Marzano." There are both imported and domestic brands on the market, as American tomato growers have cultivated the seeds and are now growing and canning them in the United States.

SUN-DRIED TOMATOES : When fresh tomatoes are dried in the sun, the result is a chewy, intensely flavored, dark red tomato. You will find sun-dried tomatoes either in jars packed in oil or dry-packed in plastic bags. We prefer to use sun-dried tomatoes packed in oil because they just need to be drained, not rehydrated, before use. We use them on pizzas where we want intense tomato flavor.

WATER

Or, should we call it "The Myth of Water?" Ask a New York pizza maker and he will tell you the secret to his dough is New York tap water. Ask a master Chicago deep-dish pizza maker and he will tell you Lake Michigan water is the key to a successful deep-dish crust. We aren't convinced. Every pizza in this book was made and tested with either Portland, Oregon, tap water or Oakland, California, tap water, and very successful results were achieved. To test the theory, Diane filled a water bottle with Chicago tap water at the O'Hare airport before a flight home. The next day she made two batches of deep-dish pizza dough, one with Portland water and the other with the Chicago water, and found no discernable difference.

YEAST

Yeast is a single-celled plant that consumes sugars and starches in a dough. As it eats, it gives off carbon dioxide gas, which causes the dough to rise, and ethanol, which gives rising bread its characteristic smell. To "proof" yeast, dissolve it in lukewarm water (90° to 100°F) before using it; high temperatures will kill the yeast.

ACTIVE DRY YEAST : Yeast in the form of tiny, dehydrated granules. The yeast cells are alive but dormant because of the lack of moisture. When combined with lukewarm water, the cells become active once again. Active dry yeast is available in ¼-ounce packages (2¼ teaspoons), in 1-pound packages, or in bulk bins at natural-foods stores. Tony prefers Red Star brand yeast at the pizzeria because of its consistently good quality and performance. Store yeast in a cool, dry place out of sunlight. It can also be refrigerated or frozen for longer storage.

FRESH CAKE YEAST : Fresh yeast comes in tiny (.6-ounce/17-gram) square cakes. Look for it in the refrigerated section of a supermarket, typically near where butter is sold; it may also be labeled "compressed fresh yeast." It is moist and very perishable and needs to be used within a week or two of purchase. Check the "use by" date on the package. It can be frozen, but should be defrosted at room temperature and used immediately. We use fresh cake yeast for our Neapolitan pizzas, as this is what is traditionally used in Naples. Our recipe for Neapolitan Pizza Dough (page 28) calls for 3 grams (½ teaspoon) of fresh cake yeast. If you open up the foil package of yeast and divide it evenly into sixths, each piece will be approximately 3 grams. For a more conventional measurement, press it lightly into a ½-teaspoon measuring spoon. (One .6-ounce package of fresh cake yeast is equal to one ¼-ounce package of active dry yeast.)

INSTANT DRY OR QUICK-RISING YEAST : Yeast in the form of very tiny, dehydrated granules. Instant dry yeast takes about half as long to leaven bread as active dry yeast or fresh cake yeast. However, for flavor preference and timing we chose to use either fresh cake yeast or active dry yeast in our recipes. If you plan to substitute instant dry yeast, use the following formulas:

If substituting for fresh cake yeast, divide the amount of fresh cake yeast by 3 for the equivalent amount of instant dry yeast. For example, a ½ teaspoon of lightly packed fresh cake yeast equals a rounded ⅛ teaspoon of instant dry yeast.

If substituting for active dry yeast, reduce the amount of active dry yeast by 20 percent for the equivalent amount of instant dry yeast. For example, one package (2¼ teaspoons) of active dry yeast equals approximately 1¾ teaspoons of instant dry yeast.

Tools for the Pizza Maker

We've made pizzas with as little as a large bowl, a wooden spoon, a knife, a pizza peel, and quarry tiles laid on the bottom rack of an oven and had spectacular results. We've also made fabulous pizzas using just about every tool on our list. We would certainly prefer to make pizzas with a full array of tools, but we have learned from our Spartan experiences that some pieces of equipment are more essential than others when making pizza at home. Review the following section and see what you may need to add to your arsenal. What you buy will depend largely on the style of pizza you're making. For instance, you won't need a pizza peel to make a deep-dish pizza; however, you will need a deep-dish pizza pan. You'll be surprised how small an investment making pizza at home requires.

TOOLS FOR MIXING

STAND MIXER : For mixing dough, the best mixer is a heavy-duty stand mixer with a dough hook attachment. We both have KitchenAid mixers with a 4½-quart mixing bowl. This size is large enough to make all of the dough recipes in this book. Use the dough hook only for mixing dough; the pastry paddle is best for making pie dough and mixing cookies and cakes.

BREAD MACHINE : Neither of us have bread machines, but many home cooks appreciate their convenience. You can mix and raise pizza dough using a bread machine. Follow the manufacturer's directions for mixing the dough and for raising times.

FOOD PROCESSOR : We don't recommend making pizza dough in a food processor because it warms up the dough too much, activating the yeast too quickly. If that is the only machine you have, however, and you don't want to make the dough by hand, then go ahead and use it; just process as minimally as possible.

BY HAND : Use a large, sturdy bowl, a wooden spoon, and all the arm muscles you have pumped up at the gym. This is actually a fun and relaxing way to make pizza dough—a real stress reducer.

TOOLS FOR PREPARING, SHAPING, AND ROLLING DOUGH

KITCHEN SCALE : We both love having a kitchen scale for weighing and portioning our dough evenly. Serious bakers weigh rather than measure their flour and other ingredients, such as cheese. Consider acquiring a scale, if you don't have one already, and getting used to measuring that way; it really helps with consistency.

DOUGH SCRAPER OR BENCHER : These are thin metal or plastic rectangular blades with either blunt or semisharp edges used to scrape or cut dough into portions. The nicer metal ones have either a rounded metal or wood handle. Use a large knife to cut dough into portions if you don't have a dough scraper.

ROLLING PIN : Use either a French-style, long, straight rolling pin without handles or a classic rolling pin with handles and, preferably, a ball-bearing rolling mechanism. If you don't have a rolling pin, you can improvise with a full wine bottle, preferably Pinot Grigio or Barolo (just kidding!). Of course, stay away from the straw-covered Chianti bottles.

DOUGH DOCKER : A dough docker is a tool with a handle and roller with prongs used to prick tiny holes in your dough so bubbles don't occur. For pizzas with a flat, non-rustic look, use a docker to prick the dough before adding the toppings.

EQUIPMENT FOR BAKING AND GRILLING PIZZAS

TONGS : Long, strong, preferably spring-loaded tongs are essential for turning food and moving the coals around when grilling. Use them for pizzas with grilled toppings; also use them to help turn or slide the crust when making grilled pizzas.

PIZZA PEEL : This is a "must have" tool for the pizza maker. Pizza peels are made of either wood or metal. The best size of peel for home use is one with a short handle about 8 inches long and a blade or surface area for the pizza that is about 14 by 15 inches. The overall length of the peel is roughly 24 inches. Wooden peels need to be treated with a food-safe oil, such as mineral oil, and should never be soaked in water. Metal peels require no maintenance. Personally, we prefer wooden peels because flour and cornmeal adhere better, providing traction for the dough to slide from the peel to the baking stone or grill grate without sticking. Plus, wooden peels have an inherent old-world charm. A large, sturdy baking sheet turned upside down works as a makeshift pizza peel.

BAKING/PIZZA STONE : The reason for using a baking stone for pizza is to create thermal mass or insulation so the oven absorbs and radiates heat evenly, increasing its effectiveness. A baking stone conducts heat like the bricks in a pizzeria brick oven. Buy the largest stone that will fit on your oven rack, either round or rectangular; the best ones are at least ½ inch thick. Pizza stones are made of porous ceramic and will stain with normal use. To clean them, use water only; soaps and detergents may transfer an unwanted taste. Stones can be cleaned in a self-cleaning oven. To prevent a pizza stone from cracking, be sure to preheat the oven with the stone already in place, and cool the stone in the oven before removing. To maximize thermal mass, preheat the oven for 45 to 60 minutes before baking pizza. You can also use two pizza stones. Keep one stone on the lowest oven rack and have another one either on the middle rack or positioned in the upper third of the oven.

UNGLAZED TILES : Unglazed tiles, such as quarry tiles, available at home centers and tile stores, are an inexpensive way to create a brick-oven effect. Buy either a 12-by-12-inch tile or six 4-by-4-inch tiles and place them side by side to create a stone. The advantage to these tiles is that they are inexpensive, so if they crack they can easily be replaced; the disadvantage is that they aren't as thick as a pizza stone.

HEARTH KIT : Perhaps the closest solution to creating a brick-oven effect in a home oven is to use a hearth kit insert. These kits, which come in three sizes, have an ideal thermodynamic design: a porous ceramic stone base and two slightly curved sidewalls. The hearth is designed to be placed on an oven rack in the upper half of the oven. The ceiling of the oven serves as the fourth wall, creating a four-walled thermal mass. When the oven door is opened, barely any heat is lost. Hearth kits are big, heavy, and expensive (about $200). Because they are big and heavy, once inserted in the oven, it is easiest to leave them in place for all baking and roasting.

PIZZA SCREENS : There are several types of pizza screens on the market: aluminum mesh–style screens, perforated-aluminum disks, and perforated-aluminum pans. All are inexpensive and come in varying sizes. Our favorite by far is the perforated-aluminum screen made by American Metalcraft. To season these screens

for optimal pizza browning, rub them on both sides with canola or grapeseed oil or vegetable-oil cooking spray and place them on the rack in a preheated 400°F oven for 30 minutes. Turn the oven off and let the screens cool in the oven. They will color and blacken over time, just as a cast-iron skillet or wok colors and seasons.

PIZZA PANS : For those who don't want to bother with a pizza peel or a pizza screen, building and baking a pizza on a pizza pan is another option. Pizza pans come in a variety of sizes and are typically made of aluminum or anodized aluminum for a better browning effect. Pizza pans with a perforated bottom help the pizza crust to crisp by releasing steam.

DEEP-DISH PIZZA PANS : Used for making Chicago-style deep-dish pizza, these pans are usually one piece; however, two-piece pans with a removable bottom are very handy for easy serving. The standard size is 14 inches in diameter and 1½ inches deep, though you can buy other sizes, including 6-inch pans to make individual pizzas. They are made of either durable heavyweight nonstick Silverstone, black baker's steel, or unglazed stoneware.

PIZZA OVENS AND GRILLS

RADIANT OVEN : For most home pizza makers, a standard electric or gas radiant oven that heats to 500° or 550°F is the norm. Making the most of your oven is what counts for turning out crackly-crisp crusts with beautifully browned bottoms and melted but not burned cheese and toppings. We have tried almost every configuration possible in terms of placement of oven racks, use of a stone, starting a pizza on an upper rack and then moving it to a stone to finish, etc. Here are our best tips:

Keep a pizza stone (or two) in the oven or use a hearth kit (see page 18). Creating thermal mass with these tools so the oven maintains its heat even when the oven door is open is crucial. The less heat lost, the better the pizza crust. The placement of a pizza stone is also important, though it varies depending on

the style of pizza being made. (Each recipe in this book specifies the placement of the oven racks and the best baking technique.)

Preheat the oven for 45 to 60 minutes. The walls and floor of the oven, plus the pizza stone, need to be as hot as possible. Even though an oven manufacturer might suggest a preheating time of, say, 15 minutes, that won't optimize the heating chamber for pizza making.

Finally, be quick and swift when opening and closing the oven door. Get the pizza in the oven quickly and try not to peek until close to the time specified for doneness in the recipes.

CONVECTION OVEN : Convection ovens, another favorite in home kitchens, are equipped with a fan that circulates the hot air around the food. We tested many of the recipes in this book using both radiant and convection ovens, and overall our best pizzas were baked in an electric radiant oven with a pizza stone. However, gas convection ovens performed better for pizza making than radiant gas ovens. In general, gas ovens have moister heat than electric ovens, so in the case of gas convection, the air circulation produces crisper crusts. If you are baking pizza in a convection oven, bake the pizzas at the maximum temperature, but adjust the baking time slightly, perhaps shaving a minute or two off the total baking time. In addition, watch for the top of the pizza baking more quickly than the bottom crust. In a convection oven, it works best to bake the pizza in the center or lower third of the oven to achieve the most even baking.

GRILL : Use either a charcoal or a gas grill (charcoal for the smokiest flavor, especially if you use hardwood lump charcoal). A simple kettle-style grill is all you need to produce delicious crackly-crisp pizzas. The trick is to have the charcoal or burners set with a hot zone and a cool zone so you can start the pizza on the hot side of the grill and finish it on the cool side. A table next to the grill is imperative for having your toppings close at hand; plus, you'll need space when you pull the pizza off the grill to add the toppings. We prefer to roll or stretch our dough in the kitchen on a solid cool surface and then transfer it to a peel for sliding onto the grill. Other helpful tools include a charcoal chimney for starting the charcoal, long tongs for moving the coals and sliding the pizza, and a metal pizza peel for sliding the dough onto the grill grate and then transferring the finished pizza to a cutting board (a metal peel won't burn if it touches the grill grate).

WOOD-FIRED OVEN : A wood-fired oven is the ultimate piece of equipment for the home pizza maker. As close to authentic as you can get, these ovens can heat from 650° to 1000°F, producing not only the high heat essential for great crusts but also a thermal mass that allows the top and the crust to cook evenly. The thick terra-cotta floor and walls absorb the heat, and the curvature of the interior oven walls and overhead crown allow for a natural convection airflow pattern. This ensures an ideal environment for baking pizza.

BRICK DECK OVEN : The serious pizza baker can now have a brick deck oven in their home. Bakers Pride electric countertop pizza ovens have two independently controlled cooking chambers with two ceramic hearth-baking decks. The brick-lined oven can heat to 650°F and is designed for top-heat intensity for that crackly-crisp crust. These can also be used for making flat breads, pretzels, and prebaked pizzas.

EQUIPMENT FOR SERVING PIZZA

PIZZA WHEEL OR CUTTER : These round knives with a rolling blade have sharp edges for cutting through crust. The handles are made of either wood, metal, or polypropylene. It's best to buy a blade that is 4 inches in diameter, so you can cut through either thin or deep-dish style pizzas.

"ROCK AND ROLL" PIZZA KNIFE : These are the Cadillac of knives for the pizza aficionado. Twenty inches long with polypropylene black handle grips on either end, they have a high-carbon steel blade that is curved on the bottom so the knife can rock back and forth for precise, clean, and crisp cutting of pizza. Dexter is a good brand to look for.

WEDGE-SHAPED SPATULA : Used for serving pies, these spatulas have a handy shape for serving wedges of pizza, too.

PIZZA PAN GRIPPER : This tool is used to handle hot pans safely. Made of either metal or professional nylon, this tool allows you to grip the pan while pulling it from the oven and also securely holds the pan in place while cutting through the pizza.

EQUIPMENT FOR EATING PIZZA

PIZZA FORK : Now we've seen it all! If either ultra-thin or deep-dish pizza is your passion, a pizza fork makes it easy to swiftly cut through crust and toppings no matter how thick or crisp. It has the same cutting wheel as a pizza cutter, along with an extra-long stainless-steel fork so you can slice and eat your pizza with one handy utensil. Try it with other foods, like pancakes, tostadas, and French toast. It's a true novelty item; your guests will love it. An easy alternative: your hands!

Dough-Tossing Techniques

Who wouldn't want to try their hand at tossing pizza dough? If supplied with a flat piece of dough and given a few simple instructions from Tony Gemignani, the five-time-world champion pizza thrower, anyone could give it a whirl—it's addictively fun. Besides, with friends, family, and children joining in, does it really matter if the first few attempts land your pizza dough on the floor or the ceiling? Like throwing a Frisbee or pitching a ball, practice may not make perfect, but it surely will help. The best dough recipes in this book for tossing are the New York–Style Pizza Dough (page 48), Tony's Pizza Dough (page 88), and the Dessert Pizza Dough (page 142). (By law and tradition, a Neapolitan *pizzaiolo* never tosses pizza dough; it is only pressed and stretched.)

Here are the steps for learning all the moves:

STEP ONE : Remove your watch and any rings you're wearing.

STEP TWO : Dust your work surface and a portion of dough lightly with flour. (A 15-ounce portion of dough, which is enough for a 12-inch pizza, is a good size for beginning throwers.)

STEP THREE : Using a rolling pin, roll the dough out into an even 8-inch round. (If the dough isn't rolled out into a circle to begin with, it won't be round in the air.) Shake the excess flour from the dough; it is now ready for tossing.

STEP FOUR : Toss the pizza in the air like you think a pizza should be thrown. Whichever direction you threw it in should be the direction you practice with—this is your natural direction for tossing. Pay attention and look at the bottom of the dough as you toss it. Did you throw it clockwise or counterclockwise? If you threw the dough clockwise, then you should toss the pizza dough with your left hand. If you threw the dough counterclockwise, use your right hand for throwing. A couple of tries will make it obvious. You always want to throw with the palm of your hand, never your knuckles.

STEP FIVE : Place the dough slightly off-center on the palm of your throwing hand. Bend your wrist back so your palm is flat (or as flat as possible; not everyone has the flexibility to bend their wrist at a ninety-degree angle). Make a fist with your other hand and place it, knuckle side up, under the dough, about 3 inches from your throwing hand; this helps to support the dough and keep it balanced and parallel to the floor. Hold the dough between your waist and chest, parallel to the ground.

STEP SIX : To release the dough, turn the palm of your throwing hand toward you, angling your elbow out slightly. With a smooth, quick motion, twist your hand outward and upward to launch the dough into the air above your head. Keep an eye on the dough and, as it comes down, catch it just below your chest with both fists, knuckles up. (It is always better to catch the dough low rather than high.) Quickly and deliberately launch the dough again, opening your fist and throwing with the palm of your hand. (If the dough is not looking round as you toss and release it, you may be tossing and catching it in the same spot. Try shifting your dough around before your next release.)

STEP SEVEN : Repeat until the dough is stretched to the desired diameter. As your pizza gets bigger, you need to spread the distance of your hands. For instance, if you are tossing a 14-inch pizza, your hands should be about 12 inches apart for the catch and release; this will prevent a weak middle.

NOTE

If the dough droops or flops, don't worry; you are probably being tentative and slow, as almost all beginners are. It takes many tries and patience to get results—but results do come, along with a lot of laughs. Just ask the champ. With a DVD and ProDough, practice "dough" that feels just like the real thing, you can practice alongside Tony. See Sources, page 160.

Throwing a Pizza Party

All you need are some friends who love pizza—even a few kids to keep things lively—and an hour or so the day before the party for dough and sauce making, and you've got the formula for a great party. We call these "full participation" parties, because your friends get to join in the pizza-making operation. You just act as general coordinator and, perhaps, oven operator—a real *pizzaiolo*.

Picture a kitchen counter laid out with bowls of assorted pizza toppings—grated cheese, pepperoni and sausage, sliced peppers and mushrooms, marinated artichokes, cooked and shredded chicken, sliced tomatoes—you get the idea. The dough operation is under control because you made several batches of dough the night before the party and it is quietly rising in the cool of the refrigerator. The pizza sauce was a cinch to make and is in a bowl with a small ladle ready for saucing the dough. You have a stack of pizza screens (inexpensive to buy—actually, downright cheap; see page 18) ready for the rolled-out dough. The oven (or ideally, two) is preheated to 500°F, with a pizza stone or two in place. An hour and a half before your guests arrive, you pull five or six portions of dough from the refrigerator—just enough to get the party started. An hour before the party, you roll and toss the dough and stretch it onto the screens. Set the screens aside on either another counter or a pizza rack—just like pizzerias use—that allows the pizzas to be vertically stacked without being smooshed.

The doorbell rings, guests arrive, and you casually and calmly offer them something to drink. Everyone "oohs" and "aahs" at all the condiments, and asks if they can make pizza, too. The extra dough in the refrigerator is ready for those guests who want to roll and toss dough. Give the kids a small portion of dough and let them make a pizza or just roll shapes and make snakes. Pair up friends, put a couple to work building a pizza—do a little matchmaking and team up two single guests to toss some dough. All the while, you're manning the oven and keeping track of the baking pizzas. Stacks of plates and paper napkins are all you need. Play a track of Dean Martin singing, "When the moon hits your eye like a big pizza pie, that's *amore* . . ." You get the idea.

PLANNING TIPS

With double ovens and two racks in each, you can make four pizzas at a time. Rotate the pizzas halfway through the baking time.

If you are planning to have children at the party and want to make individual pizzas for them, portion the dough into 8-ounce balls when you make the dough.

If you want to turn this into a grilled-pizza party, you can pre-grill the rolled-out dough on one side, set it aside on screens, and then add the toppings. Transfer the pizzas to a peel and finish the grilling when your guests arrive.

If you have a wood-fired oven (lucky you!), the pizzas will cook in just a few minutes, so raw sausage won't get cooked through. Precook any sausage toppings before assembly.

Finish with dessert pizzas (see Chapter 8), or, for simplicity, serve bowls of fruit and ice cream.

Neapolitan-Style Pizza

Pittsburgh, Pennsylvania, is not a

mecca for foodies. That's not a snob statement; that's a fact. Diane grew up in Pittsburgh and visits family there every year, checking out the food scene with each visit. There are a few ethnic gems, some local specialties like pirogies, but overall the restaurant scene is uninspiring. Except—and this should definitely be EXCEPT, in big bold letters—for an amazing, true Neapolitan pizzeria called Roberto's Pizzeria.

Owner Roberto Caporuscio is a real Neapolitan *pizzaiolo*. He studied at Associazione Verace Pizza Napoletano, a prestigious school in Naples. Roberto is the only graduate of that school here in the United States who is authorized to train and certify chefs in the skills that he learned there. In addition, he is the American president of the Associazione Pizzaioli Napoletani. His mission is to teach Americans about Italy through its regional foods.

You might ask, what are Roberto and his pizzeria doing in, of all places, Pittsburgh? It's too good to be true for a seeker of authentic food who visits the Steel City with some regularity. The short version of how Roberto ended up in Pittsburgh is that he met Sam Selario, who became his business partner, and a vision was set. Seeking to be faithful to the laws governing what can authentically be called "Neapolitan pizza," Roberto and Sam re-created a space that feels and looks just like you stepped into a pizzeria on a side street in Naples. Roberto's Pizzeria, just a few miles from downtown Pittsburgh, is in Bellevue, an old working-class neighborhood of steelworkers, dock-workers, and machinists.

The pizzeria has sand-colored, stuccoed walls with a hand-painted mural of rolling wheat fields and Italian farmhouses on one wall. The marble-topped tables from Apulia, Italy, are tightly spaced, making the pizzeria feel convivial and lively. A dozen or more twenty-five kilo bags of Caputo flour are stacked on a pallet in an alcove adding an authentic air to the casual space. The real showstopper of the pizzeria is the 4,000-pound, wood-fired brick oven Roberto brought over from Naples; he had to bulldoze and then rebuild the front of the building to get the oven inside. Decorative mosaic tiles covering the oven's dome are also the handiwork of Roberto.

The pizza oven, with an operating temperature of around 1000°F, is fueled by logs of maple, oak, and cherry. The oven's wide mouth, low arc, and thick floor and walls create a thermal mass that allows the top and bottom crusts to bake evenly and quickly—it takes 45 seconds, or a minute at the most, for a pizza to bake.

Roberto's pizzas are simple and light, with uncomplicated flavors. The crust is perfection: slightly charred with a thick rounded edge, yet with a soft, unique finish, a pleasant chew, and a slight smoky taste. The slightly thicker edge of the pizza crust is called *cornicione*, a distinct characteristic of Neapolitan pizzas.

"Food in Italy is very simple. You start with good things, you don't need a lot of them," says Caporuscio. "This is something I dreamed—explaining and sharing these traditions so Americans appreciate and understand."

This chapter is all about the glories and aesthetic simplicity of Neapolitan pizza. It reflects Roberto's patient explanations, and our understanding and true appreciation.

Neapolitan Pizza Dough

MAKES 48 OUNCES DOUGH
OR FIVE 9.5-OUNCE PORTIONS,
ENOUGH FOR FIVE 9-INCH PIZZAS

½ TEASPOON (*3 GRAMS*) FRESH
CAKE YEAST

2 CUPS LUKEWARM WATER
(*90° TO 100°F*)

1 TABLESPOON TABLE SALT OR
FINE SEA SALT

7¼ CUPS CAPUTO FLOUR, PLUS
MORE FOR DUSTING

This is Roberto Caporuscio's recipe for Neapolitan pizza dough. Diane worked side by side with Roberto, learning the finer points of making these pizzas and this dough. Although she tried to duplicate this dough using several different unbleached all-purpose American flours with 11.5 percent protein, they simply did not produce the same dough. They produced satisfactory doughs—just not with the same quality of softness, chew, crispness, and taste as using Italian Caputo flour. This flour is simply amazing. Although Caputo flour is labeled "Italian 00 flour," understand that not all 00 flours are the same (read more about Caputo flour in the Ingredient Glossary, page 13). Diane spoke with Antimo Caputo, head of the Caputo flour mill in Naples, and then spoke with Fred Mortati, the importer. With Fred's help, Diane found a source where American consumers can order this flour. See Sources, page 160.

1 In a small bowl, using a fork, stir the yeast into 1 cup of the lukewarm water. Set aside until the yeast dissolves, about 5 minutes.

2 In another small bowl, combine the salt and remaining 1 cup water. Stir to dissolve the salt.

3 To make the dough by hand: Place 7¼ cups of the flour in a large bowl. Make a well in the center of the flour and stir in the yeast mixture along with the saltwater mixture. Using a wooden spoon, mix the dough, incorporating as much of the flour as possible. Turn the dough out on a lightly floured work surface and knead until soft and elastic, 12 to 15 minutes. It will still be a little sticky but shouldn't stick to your hands. Add only a minimum amount of flour to the work surface to keep the dough from sticking.

To make the dough using a mixer: Fit a heavy-duty stand mixer with the dough hook attachment. Place 7¼ cups of the flour in the mixer bowl. Add the yeast mixture along with the saltwater mixture and mix on low speed until the flour is incorporated and the dough gathers together to form a coarse ball, about 2 minutes. Raise the speed to medium-low and mix the dough until it is smooth and not sticky, about 5 minutes longer. (If the dough begins to climb up the dough hook toward the motor drive, stop the mixer and push it down. If the machine labors and the motor feels hot, stop and wait a few minutes for the motor to cool down.) Reduce the speed to low and mix the dough for 3 minutes longer. The dough should be soft and as smooth as a baby's bottom and none of the dough should stick to the bowl. Turn the dough out on a lightly floured work surface.

4   To prepare the dough for rising: Cut the dough into fifths to form five even portions, each weighing 9.5 ounces. Pick up one portion of dough and pull the opposite edges together, wrapping them underneath toward the center to form a tight, smooth ball. Pinch to seal. Repeat with the other four portions. Place each portion in a 1-gallon lock-top plastic bag. Squeeze out all the air and seal the bags, allowing enough room for the dough to double in size.

5   Let rise in a cool room (about 60°F) for 6 to 8 hours. Alternatively, refrigerate for at least 10 hours or up to 24 hours. Remove from the refrigerator 1 hour before using to allow the dough to come to room temperature. Proceed with any Neapolitan pizza recipe.

Salsa Semplice

Simple Pizza Sauce

MAKES ABOUT 2 CUPS

2 CANS (28 OUNCES EACH) ITALIAN
PEELED TOMATOES, PREFERABLY
SAN MARZANO

1 TEASPOON SEA SALT

As you can see from the ingredient list, everything about this recipe depends on the quality of the tomatoes. The preferred tomatoes, from the famed San Marzano region of Naples, are deep red, firm, and meaty, with very few seeds. They are low in acid and high in fruitiness because they are handpicked when they are fully ripened. Although Roberto uses only imported brands, in particular the Francesconi brand, you'll find both imported and domestic brands on the market. American tomato growers have cultivated the seeds and are growing and canning San Marzano tomatoes in the United States.

In a colander or strainer, drain the tomatoes thoroughly to remove all the liquid. Crush the tomatoes lightly to remove any liquid inside the tomatoes and drain again. Transfer the tomatoes to a bowl and crush to a pulp using your hand, a potato masher, or the back of a spoon. (Alternatively, drain the tomatoes and coarsely crush the tomatoes in a food processor.) Stir in the salt. Use immediately, or store in a tightly covered container in the refrigerator for up to 5 days. Bring to room temperature before using.

Pizza Margherita

Tomato, Buffalo Mozzarella, Olive Oil, and Basil Pizza

Here is the queen of pizzas, now more than one hundred years old. This original Neapolitan pizza is made without the addition of cherry tomatoes. It's the simplicity and quality of the ingredients that make this pizza so wonderful.

MAKES ONE 9-INCH PIZZA;
SERVES 1 OR 2

1 PORTION *(9.5 OUNCES)* NEAPOLITAN PIZZA DOUGH *(PAGE 28)*, AT ROOM TEMPERATURE

CAPUTO FLOUR FOR DUSTING

¼ CUP SALSA SEMPLICE *(PAGE 30)*

2 OUNCES FRESH *MOZZARELLA DI BUFALA* OR *FIOR DI LATTE*, SQUEEZED GENTLY TO RELEASE MOISTURE, SLICED, THEN DRAINED ON PAPER TOWELS

1 TABLESPOON EXTRA-VIRGIN OLIVE OIL

4 FRESH BASIL LEAVES

1   Position an oven rack in the upper third of the oven and place a baking stone on the rack. Preheat the oven to 500°F. Have ready a pizza peel.

2   Remove the dough from the plastic bag, keeping the smooth top side facing up. Place it on a lightly floured work surface and lightly dust the dough with flour. Using your fingertips (but not your nails), press down on the dough to flatten it and push it outward into a larger circle. Flip the dough over and repeat on the other side, and then flip the dough back over. (You always want the smooth side up.)

3   Thinking of the circle of dough as a clock face, make a fist with your left hand and place it firmly at the 9 o'clock position, about 1 inch in from the edge (this will keep the edge of the dough slightly thicker). Place your right hand at the 3 o'clock position, putting your thumb on top of the dough and your other fingers under-neath. Lift the dough and stretch it a bit. Move the dough a one-eighth turn and repeat. Con-tinue until you have evenly stretched the dough into a 9-inch circle with slightly thicker edges.

4   Dust the pizza peel generously with flour. Using your hands and working quickly, lift and transfer the dough to the pizza peel. Give the peel a few shakes back and forth to make sure the dough isn't sticking.

5   To top the pizza: Spread the pizza sauce evenly over the dough, leaving a 1-inch border. Distribute the slices of mozzarella evenly over the top. Drizzle the olive oil over the cheese.

6   Give the peel another gentle shake back and forth just to make sure the dough isn't sticking. Slide the dough from the peel onto the baking stone using a quick jerking motion with your arm. (Work quickly to slide the pizza into the oven and close the door so the oven temperature doesn't drop too much.) Bake the pizza until the crust is crisp and golden brown, about 8 minutes. Using the peel, remove the pizza from the oven and transfer to a cutting board. Arrange the basil leaves like petals of a flower in the center of the pizza. Slice the pizza into wedges, or leave whole to be eaten folded in quarters, and serve immediately.

Pizza Regina Margherita

Tomato, Buffalo Mozzarella, Olive Oil, Basil, and Cherry Tomato Pizza

MAKES ONE 9-INCH PIZZA;
SERVES 1 OR 2

1 PORTION *(9.5 OUNCES)*
NEAPOLITAN PIZZA DOUGH
(PAGE 28), AT ROOM TEMPERATURE

CAPUTO FLOUR FOR DUSTING

¼ CUP SALSA SEMPLICE *(PAGE 30)*

2 OUNCES FRESH *MOZZARELLA DI BUFALA* OR *FIOR DI LATTE*, SQUEEZED GENTLY TO RELEASE MOISTURE, SLICED, THEN DRAINED ON PAPER TOWELS

8 TO 10 CHERRY TOMATOES, HALVED

1 TABLESPOON EXTRA-VIRGIN OLIVE OIL

4 FRESH BASIL LEAVES

In 1889, Regina Margherita, queen of Italy, was offered a pizza containing the colors of the Italian flag. Pizza maker Raffaele Esposito topped the pizza with tomatoes, mozzarella, and basil leaves. Faithful to the pie prepared for Queen Margherita, Roberto Caporuscio prepares this namesake pizza at his restaurant in Pittsburgh with crushed San Marzano tomatoes, buffalo mozzarella, and extra-virgin olive oil, all imported from Italy. The basil and cherry tomatoes are just like from home, grown organically and delivered by a specialty farmer.

1   Position an oven rack in the upper third of the oven and place a baking stone on the rack. Preheat the oven to 500°F. Have ready a pizza peel.

2   Remove the dough from the plastic bag, keeping the smooth top side facing up. Place it on a lightly floured work surface and lightly dust the dough with flour. Using your fingertips (but not your nails), press down on the dough to flatten it and push it outward into a larger circle. Flip the dough over and repeat on the other side, and then flip the dough back over. (You always want the smooth side up.)

3   Thinking of the circle of dough as a clock face, make a fist with your left hand and place it firmly at the 9 o'clock position, about 1 inch in from the edge (this will keep the edge of the dough slightly thicker). Place your right hand at the 3 o'clock position, putting your thumb on top of the dough and your other fingers under-neath. Lift the dough and stretch it a bit. Move the dough a one-eighth turn and repeat. Con-tinue until you have evenly stretched the dough into a 9-inch circle with slightly thicker edges.

4   Dust the pizza peel generously with flour. Using your hands and working quickly, lift and transfer the dough to the pizza peel. Give the peel a few shakes back and forth to make sure the dough isn't sticking.

5   To top the pizza: Spread the pizza sauce evenly over the dough, leaving a 1-inch border. Distribute the slices of mozzarella evenly over the top. Scatter the cherry tomatoes evenly over the top. Drizzle the olive oil over the top.

6   Give the peel another gentle shake back and forth just to make sure the dough isn't sticking. Slide the dough from the peel onto the baking stone using a quick jerking motion with your arm. (Work quickly to slide the pizza into the oven and close the door so the oven temperature doesn't drop too much.) Bake the pizza until the crust is crisp and golden brown, about 8 minutes. Using the peel, remove the pizza from the oven and transfer to a cutting board. Arrange the basil leaves like petals of a flower in the center of the pizza. Slice the pizza into wedges, or leave whole to be eaten folded in quarters, and serve immediately.

Pizza Margherita con Salame

Tomato, Buffalo Mozzarella, Salami, Olive Oil, and Basil Pizza

MAKES ONE 9-INCH PIZZA;
SERVES 1 OR 2

1 PORTION (9.5 OUNCES)
NEAPOLITAN PIZZA DOUGH
(PAGE 28), AT ROOM TEMPERATURE

CAPUTO FLOUR FOR DUSTING

¼ CUP SALSA SEMPLICE (PAGE 30)

6 THIN SLICES (ABOUT 1 OUNCE)
GENOA SALAMI

2 OUNCES FRESH MOZZARELLA
DI BUFALA OR FIOR DI LATTE,
SQUEEZED GENTLY TO RELEASE
MOISTURE, SLICED, THEN
DRAINED ON PAPER TOWELS

1 TABLESPOON EXTRA-VIRGIN
OLIVE OIL

4 FRESH BASIL LEAVES

What makes this a great little pizza is the juxtaposition of the rounded flavors of the tomatoes and mozzarella with the rich, meaty taste of salami. For this pie, Roberto uses thinly sliced Genoa salami made from pork and veal and seasoned with pepper, garlic, and red wine. If you can't find Genoa salami, use either *finocchiona* or *soppressata*.

1   Position an oven rack in the upper third of the oven and place a baking stone on the rack. Preheat the oven to 500°F. Have ready a pizza peel.

2   Remove the dough from the plastic bag, keeping the smooth top side facing up. Place it on a lightly floured work surface and lightly dust the dough with flour. Using your fingertips (but not your nails), press down on the dough to flatten it and push it outward into a larger circle. Flip the dough over and repeat on the other side, and then flip the dough back over. (You always want the smooth side up.)

3   Thinking of the circle of dough as a clock face, make a fist with your left hand and place it firmly at the 9 o'clock position, about 1 inch in from the edge (this will keep the edge of the dough slightly thicker). Place your right hand at the 3 o'clock position, putting your thumb on top of the dough and your other fingers underneath. Lift the dough and stretch it a bit. Move the dough a one-eighth turn and repeat. Continue until you have evenly stretched the dough into a 9-inch circle with slightly thicker edges.

4   Dust the pizza peel generously with flour. Using your hands and working quickly, lift and transfer the dough to the pizza peel. Give the peel a few shakes back and forth to make sure the dough isn't sticking.

5   To top the pizza: Spread the pizza sauce evenly over the dough, leaving a 1-inch border. Arrange the salami slices in a single layer over the sauce. Distribute the slices of mozzarella cheese evenly over the salami. Drizzle the olive oil over the cheese.

6   Give the peel another gentle shake back and forth just to make sure the dough isn't sticking. Slide the dough from the peel onto the baking stone using a quick jerking motion with your arm. (Work quickly to slide the pizza into the oven and close the door so the oven temperature doesn't drop too much.) Bake the pizza until the crust is crisp and golden brown, about 8 minutes. Using the peel, remove the pizza from the oven and transfer to a cutting board. Arrange the basil leaves like petals of a flower in the center of the pizza. Slice the pizza into wedges, or leave whole to be eaten folded in quarters, and serve immediately.

Pizza Mast' Nicola

Olive Oil, Pecorino Romano, and Basil Pizza

MAKES ONE 9-INCH PIZZA;
SERVES 1 OR 2

1 PORTION (*9.5 OUNCES*)
NEAPOLITAN PIZZA DOUGH
(*PAGE 28*), AT ROOM TEMPERATURE

CAPUTO FLOUR FOR DUSTING

2 TABLESPOONS EXTRA-VIRGIN
OLIVE OIL

¼ CUP FRESHLY GRATED
PECORINO ROMANO CHEESE

6 FRESH BASIL LEAVES, TORN INTO
SMALL PIECES

Pizza Mast' Nicola, or Master Nicholas's pizza, was one of the first Italian pizzas made. Instead of using olive oil, as it is now made, it was originally topped with lard. The dominant flavor of this pizza is the Pecorino Romano cheese with its intense sheep's milk flavor, peppery overtones, and distinct saltiness. The lovely counterpoint to the cheese is the soft chewy crust and the herbal aroma of freshly torn basil leaves.

1   Position an oven rack in the upper third of the oven and place a baking stone on the rack. Preheat the oven to 500°F. Have ready a pizza peel.

2   Remove the dough from the plastic bag, keeping the smooth top side facing up. Place it on a lightly floured work surface and lightly dust the dough with flour. Using your fingertips (but not your nails), press down on the dough to flatten it and push it outward into a larger circle. Flip the dough over and repeat on the other side, and then flip the dough back over. (You always want the smooth side up.)

3   Thinking of the circle of dough as a clock face, make a fist with your left hand and place it firmly at the 9 o'clock position, about 1 inch in from the edge (this will keep the edge of the dough slightly thicker). Place your right hand at the 3 o'clock position, putting your thumb on top of the dough and your other fingers underneath. Lift the dough and stretch it a bit. Move the dough a one-eighth turn and repeat. Continue until you have evenly stretched the dough into a 9-inch circle with slightly thicker edges.

4   Dust the pizza peel generously with flour. Using your hands and working quickly, lift and transfer the dough to the pizza peel. Give the peel a few shakes back and forth to make sure the dough isn't sticking.

5   To top the pizza: Brush the olive oil over the dough, leaving a 1-inch border. Evenly distribute the cheese over the oil.

6   Give the peel another gentle shake back and forth just to make sure the dough isn't sticking. Slide the dough from the peel onto the baking stone using a quick jerking motion with your arm. (Work quickly to slide the pizza into the oven and close the door so the oven temperature doesn't drop too much.) Bake the pizza until the crust is crisp and golden brown, about 8 minutes. Using the peel, remove the pizza from the oven and transfer to a cutting board. Scatter the basil evenly over the pizza. Slice the pizza into wedges, or leave whole to be eaten folded in quarters, and serve immediately.

Pizza Capricciosa

Tomato, Buffalo Mozzarella, Artichoke, Italian Baked Ham, Mushroom, and Basil Pizza

MAKES ONE 9-INCH PIZZA;
SERVES 1 OR 2

2 CREMINI MUSHROOMS, WIPED
OR BRUSHED CLEAN, STEMS
TRIMMED, SLICED ⅛ INCH THICK

2 TABLESPOONS EXTRA-VIRGIN
OLIVE OIL

SEA SALT

FRESHLY GROUND PEPPER

1 PORTION (9.5 OUNCES)
NEAPOLITAN PIZZA DOUGH
(PAGE 28), AT ROOM TEMPERATURE

CAPUTO FLOUR FOR DUSTING

Some recipes for Pizza Capricciosa call for both Italian baked ham and prosciutto. Roberto said that using just Italian baked ham is the most traditional. Look in the deli section of an Italian market or a specialty grocery store for either *prosciutto cotto* or *rosterdet prosciutto di Parma*. These Italian hams are so delicious and full-flavored we found ourselves nibbling while assembling the pizzas—buy extra!

1   Position an oven rack in the upper third of the oven and place a baking stone on the rack. Preheat the oven to 500°F. Have ready a pizza peel.

2   In a bowl, toss the mushrooms with 1 tablespoon of the olive oil and sprinkle lightly with salt and pepper. Arrange the mushrooms in a single layer in a small baking dish or ovenproof skillet. Roast the mushrooms in the preheated oven until deep brown, about 12 minutes. Transfer to a plate to cool slightly.

3   Remove the dough from the plastic bag, keeping the smooth top side facing up. Place it on a lightly floured work surface and lightly dust the dough with flour. Using your fingertips (but not your nails), press down on the dough to flatten it and push it outward into a larger circle. Flip the dough over and repeat on the other side, and then flip the dough back over. (You always want the smooth side up.)

4   Thinking of the circle of dough as a clock face, make a fist with your left hand and place it firmly at the 9 o'clock position, about 1 inch in from the edge (this will keep the edge of the dough slightly thicker). Place your right hand at the 3 o'clock position, putting your thumb on top of the dough and your other fingers underneath. Lift the dough and stretch it a bit. Move the dough a one-eighth turn and repeat. Continue until you have evenly stretched the dough into a 9-inch circle with slightly thicker edges.

5   Dust the pizza peel generously with flour. Using your hands and working quickly, lift and transfer the dough to the pizza peel. Give the peel a few shakes back and forth to make sure the dough isn't sticking.

¼ CUP SALSA SEMPLICE (*PAGE 30*)

2 OUNCES FRESH *MOZZARELLA DI BUFALA* OR *FIOR DI LATTE*, SQUEEZED GENTLY TO RELEASE MOISTURE, SLICED, THEN DRAINED ON PAPER TOWELS

1½ OUNCES THINLY SLICED ITALIAN BAKED HAM SUCH AS *PROSCIUTTO COTTO* OR *ROSTERDET PROSCIUTTO DI PARMA*

¼ CUP THICKLY SLICED MARINATED ARTICHOKE HEARTS, WELL DRAINED

4 FRESH BASIL LEAVES

6   To top the pizza: Spread the pizza sauce evenly over the dough, leaving a 1-inch border. Arrange the slices of mozzarella in a single layer over the sauce. Distribute the mushroom slices evenly over the top. Arrange the ham evenly over the mushrooms and scatter the artichoke slices over the top. Drizzle the remaining 1 tablespoon olive oil over the pizza.

7   Give the peel another gentle shake back and forth just to make sure the dough isn't sticking. Slide the dough from the peel onto the baking stone using a quick jerking motion with your arm. (Work quickly to slide the pizza into the oven and close the door so the oven temperature doesn't drop too much.) Bake the pizza until the crust is crisp and golden brown, about 8 minutes. Using the peel, remove the pizza from the oven and transfer to a cutting board. Arrange the basil leaves like petals of a flower in the center of the pizza. Slice the pizza into wedges, or leave whole to be eaten folded in quarters, and serve immediately.

Pizza Bel Paese

Beautiful Country Pizza

MAKES ONE 9-INCH PIZZA;
SERVES 1 OR 2

5 SPEARS ASPARAGUS, TOUGH
ENDS REMOVED, PEELED

2½ TABLESPOONS EXTRA-VIRGIN
OLIVE OIL

1 TEASPOON FRESH LEMON JUICE

SEA SALT

FRESHLY GROUND PEPPER

1 PORTION *(9.5 OUNCES)*
NEAPOLITAN PIZZA DOUGH
(PAGE 28), AT ROOM TEMPERATURE

CAPUTO FLOUR FOR DUSTING

2 OUNCES BEL PAESE CHEESE, CUT
INTO SIX ¼-INCH-THICK SLICES

5 THIN SLICES *(ABOUT 2 OUNCES)*
PROSCIUTTO DI PARMA

2 LARGE FRESH BASIL LEAVES

This classic and popular pizza is made with *Bel Paese* ("beautiful country") cheese, *prosciutto di Parma,* and fresh asparagus that have been roasted with olive oil, salt, pepper, and a little lemon juice. The cheese is arranged over the dough and then the prosciutto and asparagus are laid out on top like spokes on a wheel. Placed two fresh basil leaves in the center of the pizza just before it is served. *Bellissima!*

1   Position an oven rack in the upper third of the oven and place a baking stone on the rack. Preheat the oven to 500°F. Have ready a pizza peel.

2   Arrange the asparagus in a single layer in a small baking dish or ovenproof skillet. Drizzle 1½ tablespoons of the olive oil and the lemon juice over the top. Season lightly with salt and pepper. Roast until crisp-tender and nicely browned at the tips, about 12 minutes. Transfer to a plate to cool slightly.

3   Remove the dough from the plastic bag, keeping the smooth top side facing up. Place it on a lightly floured work surface and lightly dust the dough with flour. Using your fingertips (but not your nails), press down on the dough to flatten it and push it outward into a larger circle. Flip the dough over and repeat on the other side, and then flip the dough back over. (You always want the smooth side up.)

4   Thinking of the circle of dough as a clock face, make a fist with your left hand and place it firmly at the 9 o'clock position, about 1 inch in from the edge (this will keep the edge of the dough slightly thicker). Place your right hand at the 3 o'clock position, putting your thumb on top of the dough and your other fingers underneath. Lift the dough and stretch it a bit. Move the dough a one-eighth turn and repeat. Continue until you have evenly stretched the dough into a 9-inch circle with slightly thicker edges.

5   Dust the pizza peel generously with flour. Using your hands and working quickly, lift and transfer the dough to the pizza peel. Give the peel a few shakes back and forth to make sure the dough isn't sticking.

continued on page 40 →

6   To top the pizza: Drizzle the remaining 1 tablespoon olive oil over the dough, leaving a 1-inch border. Arrange the slices of cheese in a single layer over the top. Arrange the asparagus like the spokes of a wheel evenly around the pizza. Arrange a slice of prosciutto between each asparagus spear; drape the prosciutto so it curves rather than laying it perfectly flat.

7   Give the peel another gentle shake back and forth just to make sure the dough isn't sticking. Slide the dough from the peel onto the baking stone using a quick jerking motion with your arm. (Work quickly to slide the pizza into the oven and close the door so the oven temperature doesn't drop too much.) Bake the pizza until the crust is crisp and golden brown, about 8 minutes. Using the peel, remove the pizza from the oven and transfer to a cutting board. Place the basil leaves in the center of the pizza. Slice the pizza into wedges, or leave whole to be eaten folded in quarters, and serve immediately.

Pizza Marinara

Tomato, Garlic, Olive Oil, Oregano, and Basil Pizza

MAKES ONE 9-INCH PIZZA;
SERVES 1 OR 2

1 PORTION *(9.5 OUNCES)*
NEAPOLITAN PIZZA DOUGH
(PAGE 28), AT ROOM TEMPERATURE

CAPUTO FLOUR FOR DUSTING

¼ CUP SALSA SEMPLICE *(PAGE 30)*

1 LARGE CLOVE GARLIC, CUT INTO
PAPER-THIN SLICES

1 TEASPOON DRIED OREGANO

8 TO 10 CHERRY TOMATOES,
HALVED

1½ TABLESPOONS EXTRA-VIRGIN
OLIVE OIL

8 FRESH BASIL LEAVES, TORN INTO
SMALL PIECES

Around 1735, Pizza Marinara appeared, a version with cherry tomatoes, olive oil, oregano, garlic, and basil. Nothing about this recipe has changed. It is the original—very simple and full of flavor.

1   Position an oven rack in the upper third of the oven and place a baking stone on the rack. Preheat the oven to 500°F. Have ready a pizza peel.

2   Remove the dough from the plastic bag, keeping the smooth top side facing up. Place it on a lightly floured work surface and lightly dust the dough with flour. Using your fingertips (but not your nails), press down on the dough to flatten it and push it outward into a larger circle. Flip the dough over and repeat on the other side, and then flip the dough back over. (You always want the smooth side up.)

3   Thinking of the circle of dough as a clock face, make a fist with your left hand and place it firmly at the 9 o'clock position, about 1 inch in from the edge (this will keep the edge of the dough slightly thicker). Place your right hand at the 3 o'clock position, putting your thumb on top of the dough and your other fingers underneath. Lift the dough and stretch it a bit. Move the dough a one-eighth turn and repeat. Continue until you have evenly stretched the dough into a 9-inch circle with slightly thicker edges.

4   Dust the pizza peel generously with flour. Using your hands and working quickly, lift and transfer the dough to the pizza peel. Give the peel a few shakes back and forth to make sure the dough isn't sticking.

5   To top the pizza: Spread the pizza sauce evenly over the dough, leaving a 1-inch border. Distribute the slices of garlic evenly over the sauce. Crush the oregano between your fingers and sprinkle it evenly over the top. Scatter the cherry tomatoes over the sauce. Drizzle the olive oil over the top.

6   Give the peel another gentle shake back and forth just to make sure the dough isn't sticking. Slide the dough from the peel onto the baking stone using a quick jerking motion with your arm. (Work quickly to slide the pizza into the oven and close the door so the oven temperature doesn't drop too much.) Bake the pizza until the crust is crisp and golden brown, about 8 minutes. Using the peel, remove the pizza from the oven and transfer to a cutting board. Scatter the basil evenly over the pizza. Slice the pizza into wedges, or leave whole to be eaten folded in quarters, and serve immediately.

Pizza Quattro Stagioni

Four-Seasons Pizza with Artichokes, Tomatoes, Mushrooms, and Prosciutto

MAKES ONE 9-INCH PIZZA;
SERVES 1 OR 2

2 CREMINI MUSHROOMS, WIPED
OR BRUSHED CLEAN, STEMS
TRIMMED, SLICED ⅛ INCH THICK

2 TABLESPOONS EXTRA-VIRGIN
OLIVE OIL

SEA SALT

FRESHLY GROUND PEPPER

1 PORTION *(9.5 OUNCES)*
NEAPOLITAN PIZZA DOUGH
(PAGE 28), AT ROOM TEMPERATURE

CAPUTO FLOUR FOR DUSTING

With tomatoes and fresh mozzarella as the customary backdrop, this pizza has a melding of flavors that represent each season. The tomatoes symbolize summer, the mushrooms depict autumn, the intense flavors of prosciutto and salami characterize winter, and the delicate artichokes evoke spring. This is a lyrical pizza with a harmony of tastes.

1   Position an oven rack in the upper third of the oven and place a baking stone on the rack. Preheat the oven to 500°F. Have ready a pizza peel.

2   In a bowl, toss the mushrooms with 1 tablespoon of the olive oil and sprinkle lightly with salt and pepper. Arrange the mushrooms in a single layer in a small baking dish or ovenproof skillet. Roast until deep brown, about 12 minutes. Transfer to a plate to cool slightly.

3   Remove the dough from the plastic bag, keeping the smooth top side facing up. Place it on a lightly floured work surface and lightly dust the dough with flour. Using your fingertips (but not your nails), press down on the dough to flatten it and push it outward into a larger circle. Flip the dough over and repeat on the other side, and then flip the dough back over. (You always want the smooth side up.)

4   Thinking of the circle of dough as a clock face, make a fist with your left hand and place it firmly at the 9 o'clock position, about 1 inch in from the edge (this will keep the edge of the dough slightly thicker). Place your right hand at the 3 o'clock position, putting your thumb on top of the dough and your other fingers underneath. Lift the dough and stretch it a bit. Move the dough a one-eighth turn and repeat. Continue until you have evenly stretched the dough into a 9-inch circle with slightly thicker edges.

5   Dust the pizza peel generously with flour. Using your hands and working quickly, lift and transfer the dough to the pizza peel. Give the peel a few shakes back and forth to make sure the dough isn't sticking.

continued on next page →

¼ CUP SALSA SEMPLICE (*PAGE 30*)

1½ OUNCES FRESH *MOZZARELLA DI BUFALA* OR *FIOR DI LATTE*, SQUEEZED GENTLY TO RELEASE MOISTURE, SLICED, THEN DRAINED ON PAPER TOWELS

3 THIN SLICES (*ABOUT 1½ OUNCES*) *PROSCIUTTO DI PARMA*

4 THIN SLICES (*ABOUT ¾ OUNCE*) GENOA SALAMI

¼ CUP THICKLY SLICED MARINATED ARTICHOKE HEARTS, WELL DRAINED

6   To top the pizza: Spread the pizza sauce evenly over the dough, leaving a 1-inch border. Arrange the slices of mozzarella in a single layer over the sauce. Distribute the mushroom slices evenly over the top. Arrange the prosciutto and salami evenly over the mushrooms and scatter the artichoke slices over the top. Drizzle the remaining 1 tablespoon olive oil over the pizza.

7   Give the peel another gentle shake back and forth just to make sure the dough isn't sticking. Slide the dough from the peel onto the baking stone using a quick jerking motion with your arm. (Work quickly to slide the pizza into the oven and close the door so the oven temperature doesn't drop too much.) Bake the pizza until the crust is crisp and golden brown, about 8 minutes. Using the peel, remove the pizza from the oven and transfer to a cutting board. Slice the pizza into wedges, or leave whole to be eaten folded in quarters, and serve immediately.

Pizza ai Quattro Formaggi

Four-Cheese Pizza

MAKES ONE 9-INCH PIZZA;
SERVES 1 OR 2

There are many cheeses to choose from when making Pizza ai Quattro Formaggi. The cheeses chosen here are from southern Italy, but choose the Italian cheeses you like best. The cheeses should be either full-fat or semi-fat, and should vary in flavor. Try to mix so that one of the cheeses is sharp, another is mild, and another is, perhaps, smoked—you can even include a mature blue cheese. However, one of the cheeses should always be a fresh mozzarella. Talk to your local cheesemonger—ask lots of questions and taste.

1 PORTION (*9.5 OUNCES*) NEAPOLITAN PIZZA DOUGH (*PAGE 28*), AT ROOM TEMPERATURE

CAPUTO FLOUR FOR DUSTING

¾ OUNCE FRESH *MOZZARELLA DI BUFALA* OR *FIOR DI LATTE*, SQUEEZED GENTLY TO RELEASE MOISTURE, SLICED, THEN DRAINED ON PAPER TOWELS

¾ OUNCE PROVOLONE CHEESE, SLICED

¾ OUNCE SCAMORZA CHEESE, SLICED

¾ OUNCE CACIOCAVALLO CHEESE, SLICED

1 TABLESPOON FRESH ROSEMARY LEAVES

1   Position an oven rack in the upper third of the oven and place a baking stone on the rack. Preheat the oven to 500°F. Have ready a pizza peel.

2   Remove the dough from the plastic bag, keeping the smooth top side facing up. Place it on a lightly floured work surface and lightly dust the dough with flour. Using your fingertips (but not your nails), press down on the dough to flatten it and push it outward into a larger circle. Flip the dough over and repeat on the other side, and then flip the dough back over. (You always want the smooth side up.)

3   Thinking of the circle of dough as a clock face, make a fist with your left hand and place it firmly at the 9 o'clock position, about 1 inch in from the edge (this will keep the edge of the dough slightly thicker). Place your right hand at the 3 o'clock position, putting your thumb on top of the dough and your other fingers underneath. Lift the dough and stretch it a bit. Move the dough a one-eighth turn and repeat. Continue until you have evenly stretched the dough into a 9-inch circle with slightly thicker edges.

4   Dust the pizza peel generously with flour. Using your hands and working quickly, lift and transfer the dough to the pizza peel. Give the peel a few shakes back and forth to make sure the dough isn't sticking.

5   To top the pizza: Arrange the cheese slices in groups evenly over the dough, leaving a 1-inch border. Scatter half of the rosemary leaves over the top.

6   Give the peel another gentle shake back and forth just to make sure the dough isn't sticking. Slide the dough from the peel onto the baking stone using a quick jerking motion with your arm. (Work quickly to slide the pizza into the oven and close the door so the oven temperature doesn't drop too much.) Bake the pizza until the crust is crisp and golden brown, about 8 minutes. Using the peel, remove the pizza from the oven and transfer to a cutting board. Scatter the remaining rosemary leaves over the top. Slice the pizza into wedges, or leave whole to be eaten folded in quarters, and serve immediately.

CHAPTER

3

New York–Style Pizza

New York is home to the first

pizzeria in America. Credit is given to Gennaro Lombardi, who was a *pizzaiolo* in Naples before coming to New York in 1895. He worked for several years as a baker before opening Lombardi's, on Spring Street, in 1905. Lombardi's was originally a grocery, but in order to use up day-old bread Lombardi started selling "cheese pies," wrapped in paper and tied with a string. Lombardi's became a popular spot for Italian workers looking to pick up lunch and take it to work. Lombardi trained many other *pizzaioli* who went on to open their own pizzerias in New York.

Other founding fathers of pizza in New York include Anthony Pero, who established Totonno Pizzeria on Coney Island in 1924, and John Sasso, who started John's Pizza on Bleecker Street in 1929. From there, Patsy's in East Harlem opened in 1933. Other landmark pizzerias include Grimaldi's, Salvatore's, Ray's, Famous Original Ray's, RayBari Pizza, Angelo's, and Nick's. Totonno's has the distinction of being the longest-running pizzeria in the United States—and it has been run continuously by the same family for its entire history.

The stories and interconnections among the pizzerias and their owners are amazing, amusing, and legendary—especially the story of Ray's. In fact, a film called *Original* is all about the search for the original Ray's. Briefly, as the story goes, in 1959, Ralph Cuomo opened a pizzeria in Little Italy called Ray's. In the early 1960s, he opened a second place and then later sold it. It was renamed Famous Original Ray's. Several more pizzerias were opened under this new name. Then, in 1981, one of these pizzerias was sold to another guy and he changed the name to Ray's. To add yet more confusion, a fellow named Ray Bari opened a pizzeria in 1973 and called it Ray Bari Pizza. A lawsuit followed over using the name "Ray" and Ray Bari Pizza became RayBari Pizza. Now there are at least thirty pizzerias in New York with the name Ray on the sign.

So what exactly defines New York–style pizza? Lombardi's is the model from which all New York–style pizza has evolved. Unlike in Naples, where Lombardi made pizzas in a wood-fired oven, the brick ovens built in New York to bake the first pizzas were coal fired. Coal was plentiful and burned hot, creating the same intense heat as the original ovens in Naples, baking a pizza in minutes at 1000°F. Although there are still a handful of coal-fired ovens in New York, grandfathered in when the laws changed, most pizzerias today are baking their pizzas in gas or electric ovens. New York–style pizzas are thin with a chewy crust; they can be folded in half like a *libretto*, or little book, and are eaten by hand. Many say a pizza isn't New York style unless it leaves a yellow trail of oil running down to your elbow when you eat it. This comes from the fresh, whole-milk mozzarella cheese they use. The tomato sauce is thinner than most pizza sauces used, and there are only a select few ingredients that top each pizza.

Just like their peers in Chicago, with their own urban myth of water, many New York pizza makers feel you can make New York pizza only in New York because New York City tap water, a hard water, is the secret ingredient that gets the dough right.

This chapter is filled with the best re-creations of New York pizza we could find. Our dough recipe produces a crust that is flavorful, a bit chewy, and crisp. Our sauce is the classic simple, thin sauce with hints of garlic and flecks of fresh basil. The pizza combos in these recipes reflect our sense of the best New York pizza has to offer, including the New York White Pizza (page 51), the Meatball Pizza (page 54), and the Lasagna Pizza (page 57). Fire up your oven and bake away—just remember to roll up your sleeves before you fold the pizza in half and take your first bite.

New York–Style Pizza Dough

MAKES 45 OUNCES DOUGH OR
THREE 15-OUNCE PORTIONS,
ENOUGH FOR THREE
12-INCH PIZZAS

1 PACKAGE (2¼ TEASPOONS)
ACTIVE DRY YEAST

1 CUP LUKEWARM WATER
(90° TO 100°F)

1¼ CUPS ICE-COLD WATER

1 TEASPOON SUGAR

1 TABLESPOON TABLE SALT OR
1½ TABLESPOONS KOSHER SALT

2 TABLESPOONS OLIVE OIL

5¼ TO 5½ CUPS UNBLEACHED
BREAD FLOUR, PLUS MORE FOR
DUSTING

You'll find this dough to be a little wetter and tackier to work with than some of the others in the book. Learning to work with a slightly sticky dough rewards you with a crust that is crisp and airy, yet chewy. In New York, most pizza dough is pressed, stretched, and tossed, but never rolled with a rolling pin. Keep your hands well dusted with flour and even though the dough feels tacky, your hands won't stick and tear the dough. As you press and stretch the dough, if it bounces back, let it rest for a few minutes before continuing to stretch and toss the dough. This is a great dough for practicing your tossing skills! (See Dough-Tossing Techniques, pages 22–23.)

1   In a small bowl, using a fork, stir the yeast into the lukewarm water. Set aside until the yeast dissolves, about 5 minutes.

2   In another small bowl, combine the cold water, sugar, salt, and olive oil. Stir to dissolve the sugar and salt.

3   To make the dough by hand: Place 5¼ cups of the flour in a large bowl. Make a well in the center of the flour and stir in the yeast mixture along with the cold-water mixture. Using a wooden spoon, mix the dough, incorporating as much of the flour as possible. Turn the dough out on a lightly floured work surface and knead until soft and elastic, 10 to 12 minutes. It will still be a little sticky but shouldn't stick to your hands. Add only a minimum amount of flour to the work surface to keep the dough from sticking.

To make the dough using a mixer: Fit a heavy-duty stand mixer with the dough hook attachment. Place 5¼ cups of the flour in the mixer bowl. Add the yeast mixture along with the cold-water mixture and mix on low speed until the flour is incorporated and the dough gathers together to form a coarse ball, about 4 minutes. Let rest for 2 minutes and then mix on low speed until the dough is smooth and not sticky, about 6 minutes longer. (If the dough begins to climb up the dough hook toward the motor drive, stop the mixer and push it down. If the machine labors and the motor feels hot, stop and wait a few minutes for the motor to cool down.) Turn the dough out on a well-floured work surface and knead for a minute or two until it forms a smooth ball, adding up to ¼ cup of additional flour, if necessary.

4   To prepare the dough for rising: Cut the dough into thirds to form three even portions, each weighing 15 ounces. With floured hands, pick up one portion of dough and pull the opposite edges together, wrapping them underneath toward the center to form a tight, smooth ball. Pinch to seal. Repeat with the other two portions. Place each portion in a 1-gallon lock-top plastic bag. Squeeze out all the air and seal the bags, allowing enough room for the dough to double in size.

5   Refrigerate for at least 10 hours or up to 2 days. Remove from the refrigerator 1 hour before using to allow the dough to come to room temperature. Proceed with any New York–style pizza recipe.

New York–Style Pizza Sauce

MAKES ABOUT 2½ CUPS

Store-bought "pizza sauce" tends to be over-sweetened, gummy, and lacking the flavor hit of fresh herbs. Take a few minutes and make your own sauce for pizza—this one takes less than 10 minutes to come together. The good taste of imported Italian tomatoes, fruity extra-virgin olive oil, a hint of garlic, and the herbal aroma of fresh basil makes this sauce the perfect and proper base for the New York pizzas in this chapter.

1 CAN (14.5 OUNCES) DICED TOMATOES IN JUICE (SEE COOK'S NOTE)

1 CAN (6 OUNCES) TOMATO PASTE

1½ TABLESPOONS EXTRA-VIRGIN OLIVE OIL

2 TABLESPOONS CHOPPED FRESH BASIL LEAVES, OR 2 TEASPOONS DRIED BASIL

1½ TEASPOONS DRIED OREGANO

1½ TEASPOONS SUGAR

½ TEASPOON MINCED GARLIC

¾ TEASPOON TABLE SALT OR 1½ TEASPOONS KOSHER SALT

In a medium bowl, combine the diced tomatoes, including the juice from the can, the tomato paste, olive oil, basil, oregano, sugar, garlic, and salt. Taste and add more salt, if desired. Use immediately, or store in a tightly covered container in the refrigerator for up to 5 days, or freeze for up to 2 months. Bring to room temperature before using.

COOK'S NOTE

One brand of chopped tomatoes that is a favorite of ours is Pomi tomatoes, made in Italy by Parmalat. This brand of tomatoes comes in a 26.5-ounce box, which keeps the tomatoes very fresh tasting and prevents them from picking up a canned flavor. Look for them in well-stocked supermarkets or in specialty stores carrying Italian foodstuffs.

New York White Pizza

MAKES ONE 12-INCH PIZZA;
SERVES 4 TO 6

One year when Tony was in New York for the International Restaurant Convention, he and some colleagues decided to do a systematic search for the best New York white pizza. They tried at least a dozen different places. For Tony, Totonno Pizzeria is the hands-down winner for the best New York white pizza. The pizza, right out of the coal-fired brick oven, had a beautiful crisp golden crust, and the melted cheese on top was glistening white with no browned cheese spots—the benchmark for white pizza perfection.

VEGETABLE-OIL COOKING SPRAY

1 PORTION *(15 OUNCES)* NEW YORK–STYLE PIZZA DOUGH *(PAGE 48)*, AT ROOM TEMPERATURE

UNBLEACHED BREAD FLOUR FOR DUSTING

2 TABLESPOONS EXTRA-VIRGIN OLIVE OIL

¾ CUP *(ABOUT 4 OUNCES)* WHOLE-MILK RICOTTA CHEESE

1 TABLESPOON MINCED GARLIC

1¾ CUPS *(ABOUT 7 OUNCES)* COARSELY SHREDDED WHOLE-MILK, LOW-MOISTURE MOZZARELLA CHEESE

½ TEASPOON DRIED OREGANO

1   Position an oven rack on the second-lowest level in the oven and place a baking stone on the rack. Position another rack in the upper third of the oven. Preheat the oven to 500°F.

2   Coat a 12-inch pizza screen or perforated pizza pan with the cooking spray. Remove the dough from the plastic bag and place on a lightly floured work surface. Lightly dust the dough with flour into a 10-inch round. Lift the dough and check to make sure the dough isn't sticking to the work surface. Shake the excess flour from the dough. Following the Dough-Tossing Techniques on page 22, toss the dough until it is stretched to a 12-inch circle and place it on the prepared pizza screen or pan. Alternatively, lay the dough on the prepared screen or pan and gently stretch the dough into a 12-inch round.

3   To top the pizza: Brush the dough with 1 tablespoon of the olive oil. Spread the ricotta evenly over the dough, leaving a ¼-inch border. Sprinkle the garlic over the top. Scatter the mozzarella over the top. Crush the oregano between your fingers and sprinkle it evenly over the cheese and crust. Drizzle the remaining 1 tablespoon olive oil over the top.

4   Place the pizza in the oven on the upper rack. (Work quickly to slide the pizza into the oven and close the door so the oven temperature doesn't drop too much.) Bake the pizza until the crust is crisp and golden brown, 8 minutes. Using a pizza peel, lift the pizza off the screen or pan and place the crust directly on the baking stone. Using the peel or wearing thick oven mitts, remove the screen or pan from the oven. Continue baking the pizza until the bottom of the crust is golden brown, about 3 minutes longer. Using the peel, remove the pizza from the oven and transfer to a cutting board. Slice the pizza into wedges and serve immediately.

Ray's Famous Pesto and Fresh Mozzarella Pizza

MAKES ONE 12-INCH PIZZA;
SERVES 4 TO 6

There is a Ray's pizzeria in almost every neighborhood of New York. But the first and original Ray's was started in 1959 by Ralph Cuomo, on Prince Street in the heart of Little Italy. Ray's is known for their thin-crust pizzas, and their pesto and fresh mozzarella pie is one of the classics. The stretched-out dough is smeared with pesto and dotted with thin slices of fresh mozzarella. Halved ripe olives are placed in the center of each mozzarella slice. When it emerges from the oven, this pizza is a gem—an emerald pie, with a big kick of garlic and basil.

VEGETABLE-OIL COOKING SPRAY

1 PORTION (15 OUNCES)
NEW YORK–STYLE PIZZA DOUGH
(PAGE 48), AT ROOM TEMPERATURE

UNBLEACHED BREAD FLOUR FOR
DUSTING

1/3 CUP PESTO, HOMEMADE
(FACING PAGE) OR STORE-BOUGHT

1½ TABLESPOONS MINCED
GARLIC

¼ TEASPOON RED PEPPER FLAKES
(OPTIONAL)

6 OUNCES FRESH WHOLE-MILK
MOZZARELLA, THINLY SLICED AND
BLOTTED WITH PAPER TOWELS TO
REMOVE EXCESS MOISTURE

1/3 CUP HALVED AND PITTED
CANNED RIPE BLACK OLIVES

1 RIPE TOMATO, CORED AND
THINLY SLICED (OPTIONAL)

1   Position an oven rack on the second-lowest level in the oven and place a baking stone on the rack. Position another rack in the upper third of the oven. Preheat the oven to 500°F.

2   Coat a 12-inch pizza screen or perforated pizza pan with the cooking spray. Remove the dough from the plastic bag and place on a lightly floured work surface. Lightly dust the dough with flour into a 10-inch round. Lift the dough and check to make sure the dough isn't sticking to the work surface. Shake the excess flour from the dough. Following the Dough-Tossing Techniques on page 22, toss the dough until it is stretched to a 12-inch circle and place it on the prepared pizza screen or pan. Alternatively, lay the dough on the prepared screen or pan and gently stretch the dough into a 12-inch round.

3   To top the pizza: Spread the pesto evenly over the dough, leaving a ¼-inch border. Sprinkle the garlic and the red pepper flakes (if using) over the pesto. Lay the mozzarella slices evenly over the top. Place an olive half, cut side down, in the center of each cheese slice and then scatter the rest evenly over the top.

4   Place the pizza in the oven on the upper rack. (Work quickly to slide the pizza into the oven and close the door so the oven temperature doesn't drop too much.) Bake the pizza until the crust is crisp and golden brown, 8 minutes. Using a pizza peel, lift the pizza off the screen or pan and place the crust directly on the baking stone. Using the peel or wearing thick oven mitts, remove the screen or pan from the oven. Continue baking the pizza until the bottom of the crust is golden brown, about 3 minutes longer. Using the peel, remove the pizza from the oven and transfer to a cutting board. Arrange the tomato slices over the top, if desired. Slice the pizza into wedges and serve immediately.

Pesto

4 CLOVES GARLIC

1 TEASPOON KOSHER SALT

2 CUPS LIGHTLY PACKED FRESH BASIL LEAVES

½ CUP EXTRA-VIRGIN OLIVE OIL

2 TABLESPOONS TOASTED PINE NUTS *(SEE COOK'S NOTE)*

½ CUP *(2 OUNCES)* FRESHLY GRATED PARMESAN CHEESE, PREFERABLY PARMIGIANO-REGGIANO

MAKES 1 CUP

In a food processor fitted with the metal blade, process the garlic and salt until minced. Add the basil, olive oil, and pine nuts and process until smooth. Add the Parmesan and pulse just until combined. Use immediately, or store in a tightly covered container in the refrigerator for up to 2 weeks, or freeze for up to 3 months.

♟ COOK'S NOTE

To toast pine nuts, heat a small, dry, heavy-bottomed skillet over medium-high heat; when hot, add the pine nuts and stir constantly until lightly browned, about 4 minutes. Remove to a plate to cool.

Meatball Pizza

MAKES ONE 12-INCH PIZZA;
SERVES 4 TO 6

What comes forth from the oven when this pizza is done is a crisp and golden crust holding a layer of milky, melted cheese studded with large gumball-size meatballs poking through. The meatballs are bursting with herbs and spice, and the deeply flavored sauce is accented with fresh green bell pepper, onion, and a touch of garlic. Some pizzerias add pepperoni in addition to the meatballs, but, for us, this is the winning combination. The meatball recipe that follows is our favorite; you may have your own, or buy prepared meatballs if you want to save time.

VEGETABLE-OIL COOKING SPRAY

1 PORTION (15 OUNCES) NEW YORK–STYLE PIZZA DOUGH (PAGE 48), AT ROOM TEMPERATURE

UNBLEACHED BREAD FLOUR FOR DUSTING

¾ CUP NEW YORK–STYLE PIZZA SAUCE (PAGE 50)

1 TEASPOON MINCED GARLIC

2 CUPS (8 OUNCES) COARSELY SHREDDED WHOLE-MILK OR PART-SKIM, LOW-MOISTURE MOZZARELLA CHEESE

¼ CUP DICED WHITE ONION

¼ CUP DICED GREEN BELL PEPPER

10 COOKED ITALIAN-STYLE MEATBALLS (FACING PAGE)

FRESHLY GROUND PEPPER

1   Position an oven rack on the second-lowest level in the oven and place a baking stone on the rack. Position another rack in the upper third of the oven. Preheat the oven to 500°F.

2   Coat a 12-inch pizza screen or perforated pizza pan with the cooking spray. Remove the dough from the plastic bag and place on a lightly floured work surface. Lightly dust the dough with flour into a 10-inch round. Lift the dough and check to make sure the dough isn't sticking to the work surface. Shake the excess flour from the dough. Following the Dough-Tossing Techniques on page 22, toss the dough until it is stretched to a 12-inch circle and place it on the prepared pizza screen or pan. Alternatively, lay the dough on the prepared screen or pan and gently stretch the dough into a 12-inch round.

3   To top the pizza: Spread the pizza sauce evenly over the dough, leaving a ½-inch border. Sprinkle the garlic over the sauce. Scatter the mozzarella over the top. Distribute the onion and green bell pepper evenly over the cheese. Cut the meatballs in half and arrange them, cut side down, evenly over the cheese. Gently press them into the cheese. Grind fresh pepper over the top.

4   Place the pizza in the oven on the upper rack. (Work quickly to slide the pizza into the oven and close the door so the oven temperature doesn't drop too much.) Bake the pizza until the crust is crisp and golden brown, 10 minutes. Using a pizza peel, lift the pizza off the screen or pan and place the crust directly on the baking stone. Using the peel or wearing thick oven mitts, remove the screen or pan from the oven. Continue baking the pizza until the bottom of the crust is golden brown, 2 to 3 minutes longer. Using the peel, remove the pizza from the oven and transfer to a cutting board. Slice the pizza into wedges and serve immediately.

Italian-Style Meatballs

1 SLICE WHITE BREAD, CRUST REMOVED, TORN INTO TINY PIECES

2 TABLESPOONS MILK

1 POUND GROUND BEEF

½ POUND BULK MILD OR HOT ITALIAN PORK SAUSAGE

1 LARGE EGG, BEATEN

1 TABLESPOON MINCED GARLIC

½ CUP MINCED YELLOW ONION

3 TABLESPOONS MINCED FRESH FLAT-LEAF PARSLEY

3 TABLESPOONS FRESHLY GRATED PARMESAN CHEESE

1 TABLESPOON DRIED OREGANO

1 TEASPOON WORCESTERSHIRE SAUCE

1 TEASPOON KOSHER SALT

¼ TEASPOON FRESHLY GROUND PEPPER

MAKES 36 MEATBALLS

1   Preheat the oven to 450°F. Have ready a large, rimmed baking sheet, preferably nonstick.

2   In a small bowl, toss the bread with the milk and let soak for 5 minutes. Meanwhile, in a large bowl, using your hands or a heavy wooden spoon, combine the ground beef, pork sausage, egg, garlic, onion, parsley, Parmesan, oregano, Worcestershire sauce, salt, and pepper. Add the soaked bread and mix until thoroughly combined.

3   Using a spoon or small, quick-release ice-cream scoop, form the ground meat mixture into 2-inch meatballs. To make the balls smooth, wet your hands and roll them between the palms of your hand. Arrange the meatballs 1 inch apart on the baking sheet. Bake in the middle of the oven until nicely browned and cooked through, about 20 minutes. Cut into one to check for doneness.

COOK'S NOTE

Cooked meatballs may be refrigerated, covered, for up to 3 days, or frozen for up to 2 months. Thaw frozen meatballs for about 24 hours in the refrigerator. Warm in a preheated 300°F oven before serving.

Lasagna Pizza

MAKES ONE 12-INCH PIZZA;
SERVES 4 TO 6

2 TEASPOONS KOSHER SALT

3 STRIPS DRIED LASAGNA NOODLES

½ TABLESPOON ROASTED
GARLIC–FLAVORED OLIVE OIL

VEGETABLE-OIL COOKING SPRAY

1 PORTION (15 OUNCES)
NEW YORK–STYLE PIZZA DOUGH
(PAGE 48), AT ROOM TEMPERATURE

UNBLEACHED BREAD FLOUR FOR
DUSTING

Before Tony even knew there was lasagna pizza on a Ray's menu in New York, he had created a lasagna pizza for his pizzeria Pyzano's in Castro Valley, California. Not your usual pie, this one is layered, just like lasagna, starting with ricotta and then sauce over the dough. Next, cooked lasagna noodles are arranged on top, more sauce is added, Parmesan and garlic are sprinkled over the sauce, sausage is dotted over the sauce, and cheese is spread over it all. Think about making this pizza when you have leftover pasta. There's even a New York pizza called "Ziti with Meat Sauce Pie."

1   Position an oven rack on the second-lowest level in the oven and place a baking stone on the rack. Position another rack in the upper third of the oven. Preheat the oven to 500°F.

2   While the oven is heating, fill a large saucepan two-thirds full of water, cover, and bring to a boil over high heat. Add the salt and then add the lasagna noodles. Stir to submerge the noodles and cook until al dente (cooked through but still slightly chewy), about 10 minutes. Drain in a colander, rinse under cold water, drain again, and blot dry. Brush the noodles on both sides with the olive oil. Cut several 1-inch-long slits lengthwise down the center of the noodles. Set aside.

3   Coat a 12-inch pizza screen or perforated pizza pan with the cooking spray. Remove the dough from the plastic bag and place on a lightly floured work surface. Lightly dust the dough with flour into a 10-inch round. Lift the dough and check to make sure the dough isn't sticking to the work surface. Shake the excess flour from the dough. Following the Dough-Tossing Techniques on page 22, toss the dough until it is stretched to a 12-inch circle and place it on the prepared pizza screen or pan. Alternatively, lay the dough on the prepared screen or pan and gently stretch the dough into a 12-inch round.

continued on next page →

¾ CUP (*ABOUT 4 OUNCES*) WHOLE-MILK RICOTTA CHEESE

1 CUP NEW YORK–STYLE PIZZA SAUCE (*PAGE 50*)

2 TABLESPOONS FRESHLY GRATED PARMESAN CHEESE

1 TEASPOON MINCED GARLIC

½ POUND BULK MILD OR HOT ITALIAN PORK SAUSAGE, SEPARATED INTO SMALL CHUNKS

2 CUPS (*8 OUNCES*) COARSELY SHREDDED WHOLE-MILK OR PART-SKIM, LOW-MOISTURE MOZZARELLA CHEESE

1½ TEASPOONS DRIED OREGANO

4   To top the pizza: Spread the ricotta evenly over the dough, leaving a ½-inch border. Spoon ½ cup of the pizza sauce evenly over the ricotta. Lay the lasagna noodles over the sauce, trimming the noodles to fit. Fill in any spaces with the trimmings. Spoon the remaining ½ cup pizza sauce over the noodles and then sprinkle the Parmesan and garlic over the top. Distribute the chunks of sausage over the sauce. Scatter the mozzarella over the top. Crush the oregano between your fingers and sprinkle it evenly over the cheese and crust.

5   Place the pizza in the oven on the upper rack. (Work quickly to slide the pizza into the oven and close the door so the oven temperature doesn't drop too much.) Bake the pizza until the crust is crisp and golden brown, 10 minutes. Using a pizza peel, lift the pizza off the screen or pan and place the crust directly on the baking stone. Using the peel or wearing thick oven mitts, remove the screen or pan from the oven. Continue baking the pizza until the bottom of the crust is golden brown, 3 to 4 minutes longer. Using the peel, remove the pizza from the oven and transfer to a cutting board. Slice the pizza into wedges and serve immediately.

Tribute Pizza for Lombardi's Tomato and Sliced Mozzarella Pie

MAKES ONE 12-INCH PIZZA;
SERVES 4 TO 6

1 PORTION *(15 OUNCES)* NEW YORK–STYLE PIZZA DOUGH *(PAGE 48)*, AT ROOM TEMPERATURE

FLOUR AND MEDIUM-GRIND YELLOW CORNMEAL FOR DUSTING

½ CUP NEW YORK–STYLE PIZZA SAUCE *(PAGE 50)*, PURÉED UNTIL SMOOTH

½ TABLESPOON FRESHLY GRATED PARMESAN CHEESE

10 THIN SLICES *(6 OUNCES)* WHOLE-MILK, LOW-MOISTURE MOZZARELLA CHEESE

1 TABLESPOON EXTRA-VIRGIN OLIVE OIL

¼ TEASPOON DRIED OREGANO *(OPTIONAL)*

Gennaro Lombardi, a true *pizzaiolo* from Naples, is considered the founding father of pizza in America. He started selling pizza in New York City in 1897 and opened the first pizzeria, called Lombardi's, in 1905. This is the simple Neapolitan-style, Margherita pizza he made back home in Naples.

1   Position an oven rack in the upper third of the oven and place a baking stone on the rack. Preheat the oven to 500°F. Have ready a pizza peel.

2   Remove the dough from the plastic bag and place on a lightly floured work surface. Lightly dust the dough with flour into a 10-inch round. Lift the dough and check to make sure the dough isn't sticking to the work surface. Shake the excess flour from the dough. Following the Dough-Tossing Techniques on page 22, toss the dough until it is stretched to a 12-inch circle. Alternatively, gently stretch the dough into a 12-inch round.

3   Dust the pizza peel generously with cornmeal. Using your hands and working quickly, lift and transfer the dough to the pizza peel. Give the peel a few shakes back and forth to make sure the dough isn't sticking.

4   To top the pizza: Spread the pizza sauce evenly over the dough, leaving a ½-inch border. Sprinkle the Parmesan over the sauce. Distribute the mozzarella slices evenly over the top. Drizzle the olive oil over the cheese. Crush the oregano between your fingers and sprinkle it evenly over the cheese and crust, if desired.

5   Give the peel another gentle shake back and forth just to make sure the dough isn't sticking. Slide the dough from the peel onto the baking stone using a quick jerking motion with your arm. (Work quickly to slide the pizza into the oven and close the door so the oven temperature doesn't drop too much.) Bake the pizza until the crust is crisp and golden brown, 10 minutes. Using the peel, remove the pizza from the oven and transfer to a cutting board. Slice the pizza into wedges and serve immediately.

Spinach and Ricotta Pizza

MAKES ONE 12-INCH PIZZA;
SERVES 4 TO 6

VEGETABLE-OIL COOKING SPRAY

1 PORTION *(15 OUNCES)*
NEW YORK–STYLE PIZZA DOUGH
(PAGE 48), AT ROOM TEMPERATURE

UNBLEACHED BREAD FLOUR FOR
DUSTING

2 TABLESPOONS EXTRA-VIRGIN
OLIVE OIL

½ CUP NEW YORK–STYLE PIZZA
SAUCE *(PAGE 50)*

½ TABLESPOON FRESHLY GRATED
PARMESAN CHEESE

1½ CUPS *(1½ OUNCES)* LIGHTLY
PACKED FRESH SPINACH LEAVES,
TORN INTO LARGE PIECES

½ TEASPOON MINCED FRESH
GARLIC

A true slice of heaven is eating a New York spinach and ricotta pie. Extra-virgin olive oil is drizzled over the dough, then a smearing of sauce and a sprinkling of garlic are added before fresh, coarsely torn spinach is layered on top. Whole-milk mozzarella is the protective cover that keeps the spinach from burning, and little globs of ricotta dot the pie. It's a classic.

1   Position an oven rack on the second-lowest level in the oven and place a baking stone on the rack. Position another rack in the upper third of the oven. Preheat the oven to 500°F.

2   Coat a 12-inch pizza screen or perforated pizza pan with the cooking spray. Remove the dough from the plastic bag and place on a lightly floured work surface. Lightly dust the dough with flour into a 10-inch round. Lift the dough and check to make sure the dough isn't sticking to the work surface. Shake the excess flour from the dough. Following the Dough-Tossing Techniques on page 22, toss the dough until it is stretched to a 12-inch circle and place it on the prepared pizza screen or pan. Alternatively, lay the dough on the prepared screen or pan and gently stretch the dough into a 12-inch round.

3   To top the pizza: Brush the dough with 1 tablespoon of the olive oil. Spread the pizza sauce evenly over the dough, leaving a ¼-inch border. Sprinkle the Parmesan over the top. Scatter the spinach over the top and sprinkle the garlic over the spinach. Cover the spinach with the mozzarella. Using a teaspoon or your fingers, arrange little globs of ricotta evenly over the top. Drizzle the remaining 1 tablespoon olive oil over the top.

continued on next page →

2 CUPS *(8 OUNCES)* COARSELY SHREDDED WHOLE-MILK OR PART-SKIM, LOW-MOISTURE MOZZARELLA CHEESE

⅓ CUP *(3 OUNCES)* WHOLE-MILK RICOTTA CHEESE

1 RIPE TOMATO, CORED AND THINLY SLICED *(OPTIONAL)*

4   Place the pizza in the oven on the upper rack. (Work quickly to slide the pizza into the oven and close the door so the oven temperature doesn't drop too much.) Bake the pizza until the crust is crisp and golden brown, 10 minutes. Using a pizza peel, lift the pizza off the screen or pan and place the crust directly on the baking stone. Using the peel or wearing thick oven mitts, remove the screen or pan from the oven. Continue baking the pizza until the bottom of the crust is golden brown, about 3 minutes longer. Using the peel, remove the pizza from the oven and transfer to a cutting board. Arrange the tomato slices over the top, if desired. Slice the pizza into wedges and serve immediately.

Italian Sausage and Three Pepper Pizza

MAKES ONE 12-INCH PIZZA;
SERVES 4 TO 6

2 TABLESPOONS OLIVE OIL

1 SMALL GREEN BELL PEPPER,
SEEDED, DERIBBED, AND CUT
INTO ¼-INCH STRIPS

1 SMALL RED BELL PEPPER,
SEEDED, DERIBBED, AND CUT
INTO ¼-INCH STRIPS

1 SMALL YELLOW BELL PEPPER,
SEEDED, DERIBBED, AND CUT
INTO ¼-INCH STRIPS

1 TEASPOON MINCED GARLIC

½ TEASPOON DRIED OREGANO

¼ TEASPOON CAYENNE PEPPER

½ TEASPOON KOSHER SALT

FRESHLY GROUND BLACK PEPPER

VEGETABLE-OIL COOKING SPRAY

In the Italian tradition, sausage and peppers were standard fare for an easy weeknight meal. So it makes sense for a pizza to be colorfully topped with chunks of sausage and a medley of sweet peppers. Not wanting the peppers to taste raw, we chose to quickly sauté them with a hint of garlic, oregano, and a kick of cayenne. The peppers are then layered over our flavor-packed pizza sauce, topped with chunks of spicy sausage, covered with cheese, and baked to perfection. More top-heavy than our other New York pies, this pizza may be a little harder to fold like a book, but we promise it will leave an oozing trail of oil down your arm!

1   Position an oven rack on the second-lowest level in the oven and place a baking stone on the rack. Position another rack in the upper third of the oven. Preheat the oven to 500°F.

2   While the oven is heating, warm the olive oil in a large skillet, preferably nonstick, over medium-high heat. Add all the bell peppers and sauté, stirring frequently, until crisp-tender, about 4 minutes. Add the garlic, oregano, cayenne, salt, and a few grindings of fresh black pepper and sauté for 1 minute longer. Set aside to cool slightly.

3   Coat a 12-inch pizza screen or perforated pizza pan with the cooking spray. Remove the dough from the plastic bag and place on a lightly floured work surface. Lightly dust the dough with flour into a 10-inch round. Lift the dough and check to make sure the dough isn't sticking to the work surface. Shake the excess flour from the dough. Following the Dough-Tossing Techniques on page 22, toss the dough until it is stretched to a 12-inch circle and place it on the prepared pizza screen or pan. Alternatively, lay the dough on the prepared screen or pan and gently stretch the dough into a 12-inch round.

4   To top the pizza: Spread the pizza sauce evenly over the dough, leaving a ½-inch border. Distribute the peppers over the sauce. Arrange the sausage slices over the top. Scatter the moz-zarella over the top. Arrange the chunks of bulk sausage evenly over the cheese, pressing them into the cheese slightly.

continued on page 65 →

1 PORTION *(15 OUNCES)* NEW YORK–STYLE PIZZA DOUGH *(PAGE 48)*, AT ROOM TEMPERATURE

UNBLEACHED BREAD FLOUR FOR DUSTING

½ CUP NEW YORK–STYLE PIZZA SAUCE *(PAGE 50)*

2 MILD OR HOT ITALIAN PORK SAUSAGES *(ABOUT ½ POUND)*, CUT CROSSWISE INTO ¼-INCH SLICES

2 CUPS *(8 OUNCES)* COARSELY SHREDDED WHOLE-MILK OR PART-SKIM, LOW-MOISTURE MOZZARELLA CHEESE

¼ POUND BULK MILD OR HOT ITALIAN PORK SAUSAGE, SEPARATED INTO SMALL CHUNKS

½ TABLESPOON FRESHLY GRATED PARMESAN CHEESE

5   Place the pizza in the oven on the upper rack. (Work quickly to slide the pizza into the oven and close the door so the oven temperature doesn't drop too much.) Bake the pizza until the crust is crisp and golden brown, 10 minutes. Using a pizza peel, lift the pizza off the screen or pan and place the crust directly on the baking stone. Using the peel or wearing thick oven mitts, remove the screen or pan from the oven. Continue baking the pizza until the bottom of the crust is golden brown, 3 to 4 minutes longer. Using the peel, remove the pizza from the oven and transfer to a cutting board. Sprinkle the Parmesan over the top. Slice the pizza into wedges and serve immediately.

CHAPTER

4

Chicago-Style Deep-Dish Pizza

"So, where are you going to get Lake Michigan water?" That was the question posed to Diane when she interviewed Jim Freeland, corporate chef of the famed Lou Malnati's pizzerias in Chicago. Jim swears that the true secret to making a truly delicious Chicago-style deep-dish pizza crust is in the water. He also swears by all the rest of the fine ingredients that make up a Chicago deep-dish pie.

Although charming and talkative, Jim certainly wasn't forthcoming with recipes or sources of ingredients. It's all part of the mystique of Chicago pizza. When asked about the tomatoes, Jim would only say that they have special growers in California. Every year he and the Malnati brothers travel to California to taste the tomatoes. Only the finest vine-ripened plum tomatoes are then blended and canned exclusively for the Malnati's pizzerias. Asked about the cheese, Jim said the mozzarella has been handmade by the same dairy for three decades. Diane suggested the dairy might be in Wisconsin; Jim would only say it was in the Upper Midwest. "Tell me about the sausage?" asked Diane. "We grind our own sausage and it's 90 percent lean. They only make it for us," Jim responded. Diane's final question to Jim was, "So, is the recipe for the dough written down?" Jim said, "I know it, but otherwise it's in the vault." Like a good poker player, Jim was cagey and sly, yet kind, enjoying having the upper hand in the conversation.

Diane has played around in the kitchen trying to duplicate these famed deep-dish pizzas since 1978, when Edwardo's, another famous Chicago pizzeria, opened in Hyde Park. Diane and her husband, Greg, then a graduate student at the University of Chicago, ate deep-dish pizza often—part of the poor-student's diet. Unlike Lou Malnati's, Pizzeria Uno, or Pizzeria Due, Edwardo's had a full display of ingredients piled high in baskets as you entered the restaurant. Proudly displayed were plump and ripe plum tomatoes, bushels of peppers, bags of onions, and pots of basil plants growing in the window. Edwardo's is best known for its innovative two-inch-high stuffed pizza loaded with cheese and fresh spinach, and topped with a light crust. Along with deep-dish, stuffed pizzas are another Chicago hallmark.

Briefly, the whole tale of deep-dish pizza started with Ike Sewell in 1941, when Pizzeria Uno opened in downtown Chicago. In 1955, Ike opened Pizzeria Due across the street to handle the crowds. In 1966, two cab drivers decided to open Gino's East and hired away (stole?) a pizza cook from Pizzeria Uno. Lou Malnati, manager of the original Pizzeria Uno for twenty-two years, moved to the suburbs and opened Lou Malnati's Pizzerias. Now his sons, Marc and Rick, run the restaurants. As of the writing of this book, there are 191 Pizzeria Uno's in 34 states. Lou Malnati now has 21 pizzerias. Edwardo's has 11 locations in 3 states and Gino's has 10 locations. Another revered deep-dish style pizzeria, Giordano's, opened in 1974 and has 39 locations in Illinois, plus 2 pizzerias in Florida.

There is an intense, legendary rivalry existing between New Yorkers and Chicagoans, each defending their styles of pizza with gusto, bravura, and pride. Chicagoans say eating New York pizza is like eating ketchup on cardboard. To New Yorkers, if you can't pick it up and fold it like a book, it ain't pizza—eating pizza with a knife and fork doesn't make sense to them. As lovers of all things pizza, Chicago-style pizza makes sense to us. This chapter offers those thick pizzas, oozing with cheese, vegetables, and sausage. It took a little espionage to get the recipes, but we did it!

Chicago-Style Deep-Dish Pizza Dough

MAKES 30 OUNCES DOUGH,
ENOUGH FOR ONE
14-INCH DEEP-DISH PIZZA OR
ONE 9-INCH STUFFED PIZZA

1 PACKAGE *(2¼ TEASPOONS)* ACTIVE DRY YEAST

1¼ CUPS LUKEWARM WATER *(90° TO 100°F)*

1 TEASPOON SUGAR

3¼ CUPS UNBLEACHED BREAD FLOUR, PLUS MORE FOR DUSTING

½ CUP MEDIUM-GRIND YELLOW CORNMEAL

1 TEASPOON TABLE SALT OR 1½ TEASPOONS KOSHER SALT

¼ CUP OLIVE OIL, PLUS MORE FOR OILING BOWL AND PAN

Ever since Diane tasted her first deep-dish in 1978 at Pizzeria Uno in Chicago, she set herself the goal of figuring out the recipe for the crust. After years of experimentation and hundreds of deep-dish pizzas, we think this is as authentic a recipe for deep-dish pizza crust as you will find. Of course, use Lake Michigan water if you can (!), but, otherwise, regular tap water will do just fine. It is the combination of the flour and crunchy cornmeal and the addition of oil that gives this crust its signature qualities: both light and crispy at the edges. Unlike New York– or California-style pizzas, this dough is never rolled. Use lightly oiled fingertips to gently press the dough into the pan. If the dough springs back, let it rest for a few minutes and then gently press again without pulling and stretching. This pressing technique allows the dough to develop a delicate biscuitlike structure.

1   To make the dough by hand: Begin by making a sponge. In a large bowl, dissolve the yeast in ¼ cup of the warm water. Add the sugar and ¼ cup of the flour and stir with a wooden spoon or rubber spatula to combine. Cover with plastic wrap and let rise in a warm place for 20 minutes. Add the remaining 1 cup warm water and 3 cups flour, the cornmeal, salt, and ¼ cup olive oil. Using a wooden spoon, mix the dough, incorporating as much of the flour as possible. Turn the dough out on a lightly floured work surface and knead until soft and elastic, 10 to 12 minutes. It will still be a little sticky but shouldn't stick to your hands. Add only a minimum amount of flour to the work surface to keep the dough from sticking. Lightly oil a large bowl. Add the dough and turn to coat on all sides. Cover the bowl with plastic wrap and place a clean, damp kitchen towel over the top.

To make the dough using a mixer: Begin by making a sponge. Fit a heavy-duty stand mixer with the dough hook attachment. In the mixer bowl, combine the yeast with ¼ cup of the warm water, then add the sugar and ¼ cup of the flour. Mix on low speed until combined. Place a clean, damp kitchen towel over the mixer to cover the bowl and let the sponge rise for 20 minutes. Add the remaining 1 cup warm water and 3 cups flour, the cornmeal, salt, and ¼ cup olive oil. Mix on low speed until the flour is incorporated and the dough gathers together to form a coarse ball, about 4 minutes. Let rest for 2 minutes, then mix on medium-low speed until the dough is smooth and slightly sticky, about 3 minutes longer. Even if the dough seems too sticky, turn the dough out on a well-floured work surface and knead for a minute or two until it forms a smooth ball, adding up to ¼ cup of additional flour, if necessary.

Lightly oil a large bowl (or use the mixer bowl), add the dough, and turn to coat on all sides.

2   Set the bowl in a warm spot (a pilot-heated oven is a good spot, or an electric oven turned to 150°F for 5 minutes and then turned off). Let the dough rise until doubled in volume, 1½ to 2 hours. (For a slow rise, place the covered bowl in the refrigerator and let the dough rise for 10 to 12 hours. Bring the dough to room temperature before completing the final rise.)

3   When the dough has doubled in volume, punch it down and knead it for 2 to 3 minutes. Press the dough evenly into the bottom of an oiled 14-inch round deep-dish pizza pan (see recipe introduction). Let the dough rise in the pan for 15 to 20 minutes. Press the dough until it comes 2 inches up the sides and is even on the bottom and at the corners of the pan. Proceed with any deep-dish pizza recipe.

Chicago-Style Butter-and-Garlic Deep-Dish Pizza Dough

MAKES 30 OUNCES DOUGH, ENOUGH FOR ONE 14-INCH DEEP-DISH PIZZA OR ONE 9-INCH STUFFED PIZZA

1 PACKAGE (2¼ TEASPOONS) ACTIVE DRY YEAST

1¼ CUPS LUKEWARM WATER (90° TO 100°F)

1 TEASPOON SUGAR

3¼ CUPS UNBLEACHED BREAD FLOUR, PLUS MORE FOR DUSTING

½ CUP MEDIUM-GRIND YELLOW CORNMEAL

1 TEASPOON TABLE SALT OR 1½ TEASPOONS KOSHER SALT

¼ CUP UNSALTED BUTTER, MELTED

1 CLOVE GARLIC, MINCED TO A PASTE

VEGETABLE OIL FOR OILING THE BOWL AND PAN

A variation on the deep-dish crust is to use melted butter instead of oil in the dough to achieve a golden crust that is light and especially crispy. The addition of minced garlic flavors the crust in a subtle but delicious way—the more garlic the better. We especially like to use this crust when making the combo vegetable deep-dish pizzas and the spinach-and-mozzarella version. Lou Malnati's makes a dynamite butter-crust deep-dish pizza. A lot of sleuthing (and eating) was involved in figuring out this recipe!

1   To make the dough by hand: Begin by making a sponge. In a large bowl, dissolve the yeast in ¼ cup of the warm water. Add the sugar and ¼ cup of the flour and stir with a wooden spoon or rubber spatula to combine. Cover with plastic wrap and allow to rise in a warm place for 20 minutes. Add the remaining 1 cup warm water and 3 cups flour, the cornmeal, and salt. Combine the butter and garlic and add it to the sponge. Using a wooden spoon, mix the dough, incorporating as much of the flour as possible. Turn the dough out on a lightly floured work surface and knead until soft and elastic, 10 to 12 minutes. It will still be a little sticky but shouldn't stick to your hands. Add only a minimum amount of flour to the work surface to keep the dough from sticking. Lightly oil a large bowl. Add the dough and turn to coat on all sides. Cover the bowl with plastic wrap and place a clean, damp kitchen towel over the top.

To make the dough using a mixer: Begin by making a sponge. Fit a heavy-duty stand mixer with the dough hook attachment. In the mixer bowl, combine the yeast with ¼ cup of the warm water, then add the sugar and ¼ cup of the flour. Mix on low speed until combined. Place a clean, damp kitchen towel over the mixer to cover the bowl and let the sponge rise for 20 minutes. Add the remaining 1 cup warm water and 3 cups flour, the cornmeal, and salt. Combine the butter and garlic and add it to the sponge. Mix on low speed until the flour is incorporated and the dough gathers together to form a coarse ball, about 4 minutes. Let rest for 2 minutes, then mix on medium-low speed until the dough is smooth and slightly sticky, about 3 minutes longer. Even if the dough seems too sticky, turn the dough out on a well-floured work surface and knead for a minute or two until it forms a smooth ball, adding up to ¼ cup of additional flour, if necessary. Lightly oil a large bowl (or use the mixer bowl), add the dough, and turn to coat on all sides.

2   Set the bowl in a warm spot (a pilot-heated oven is a good spot, or an electric oven turned to 150°F for 5 minutes and then turned off). Let the dough rise until doubled in volume, 1½ to 2 hours. (For a slow rise, place the covered bowl in the refrigerator and let the dough rise for 10 to 12 hours. Bring the dough to room temperature before completing the final rise.)

3   When the dough has doubled in volume, punch it down and knead it for 2 to 3 minutes. Press the dough evenly into the bottom of an oiled 14-inch round deep-dish pizza pan (see recipe introduction, page 68). Let the dough rise in the pan for 15 to 20 minutes. Press the dough until it comes 2 inches up the sides and is even on the bottom and at the corners of the pan. Proceed with any deep-dish pizza recipe.

Slow-Simmered Tomato Sauce for Deep-Dish Pizza

MAKES 3½ CUPS

2 CANS (28 OUNCES EACH) WHOLE ITALIAN-STYLE PEELED TOMATOES

1 TABLESPOON DRIED OREGANO

1 TEASPOON KOSHER SALT

2 CLOVES GARLIC, MINCED

8 LARGE FRESH BASIL LEAVES, COARSELY CHOPPED

½ TEASPOON RED PEPPER FLAKES (OPTIONAL)

There are lots of versions of tomato sauce used to make Chicago-style deep-dish pizza. Some pizzerias use cooked sauces, some make simple uncooked sauces by draining and crushing canned tomatoes and adding olive oil and herbs. For the Chicago deep-dish pizzas in this chapter, we chose a slow-simmered sauce that starts with canned crushed tomatoes that are cooked down to produce a thick, rich-tasting sauce. A combination of dried and fresh herbs is added, along with a big kick of garlic. Add red pepper flakes if you like; we especially liked them with the spinach deep-dish pizzas.

Place the tomatoes, including the juice from the cans, in a large saucepan. Crush the tomatoes using the back of a large spoon or squish them with your hand. Stir in the oregano and salt. Simmer the tomatoes, uncovered, over medium-low heat until the sauce is thick and all the liquid has evaporated, about 50 minutes. Remove from the heat and let cool. Stir in the garlic and basil. Add the red pepper flakes, if desired. Use immediately, or refrigerate in a tightly covered container for up to 3 days, or freeze for up to 2 months. Bring to room temperature before using.

Deep-Dish Pizza with Sausage, Garlic, and Mozzarella

MAKES ONE 14-INCH DEEP-DISH
PIZZA; SERVES 4 TO 6

1½ TABLESPOONS OLIVE OIL

CHICAGO-STYLE DEEP-DISH PIZZA
DOUGH *(PAGE 68)*, AT ROOM
TEMPERATURE

1 POUND MILD OR HOT ITALIAN
PORK SAUSAGE, CASINGS
REMOVED, CRUMBLED

1 POUND WHOLE-MILK OR
PART-SKIM, LOW-MOISTURE
MOZZARELLA, THINLY SLICED

2 CLOVES GARLIC, MINCED

3½ CUPS SLOW-SIMMERED
TOMATO SAUCE *(PAGE 72)*, AT
ROOM TEMPERATURE

½ CUP *(2 OUNCES)* FRESHLY
GRATED PARMESAN CHEESE

Ideally, buy top-quality Italian pork sausages from a meat market that makes their own sausages; or buy packaged sausages that contain no filler or preservatives. Most of the Chicago-style pizzerias use raw sausage in their deep-dish pizzas. This does not work as well for the home cook for two reasons: First, commercial pizzerias, with their low, deep, well-insulated ovens, are able to cook pizzas so the filling is completely cooked through without over-browning the crust and top of the pizza. Second, the sausage they are able to buy is very lean, usually 90 percent lean pork meat, so it doesn't ooze excess fat into the pizza. The best choice for the home cook is to precook the sausage and drain off the excess fat. This is hardly a compromise—wait 'til you taste this pizza!

1   Position an oven rack on the second-lowest level in the oven and place a baking stone, if using one, on the rack. Preheat the oven to 500°F.

2   Brush a 14-inch round deep-dish pizza pan with ½ tablespoon of the olive oil. Starting in the middle and using your fingertips, press the dough evenly to cover the bottom and about 2 inches up the sides of the pan. Cover the pan with plastic wrap or a clean kitchen towel and let the dough rise in the pan for 15 to 20 minutes.

3   Meanwhile, in a large skillet over medium heat, warm the remaining 1 tablespoon olive oil and swirl to coat the plan. Scatter the sausage in the pan and sauté, stirring frequently, until the sausage is cooked through and no longer pink,

about 5 minutes. Remove the pan from the heat. Using a slotted spoon, drain the sausage of all excess fat and transfer the sausage to a plate.

4   To assemble the pizza, lightly press the dough up the sides of the pan if it has slid back down. Lay half of the mozzarella slices over the pizza dough, overlapping them to cover the dough completely. Scatter the cooked sausage over the top. Sprinkle the garlic over the sausage. Arrange the rest of the mozzarella over the top of the sausage and garlic. Ladle the tomato sauce evenly over the mozzarella. Sprinkle the Parmesan over the top of the sauce.

continued on next page ➡

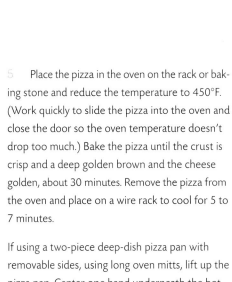

5   Place the pizza in the oven on the rack or baking stone and reduce the temperature to 450°F. (Work quickly to slide the pizza into the oven and close the door so the oven temperature doesn't drop too much.) Bake the pizza until the crust is crisp and a deep golden brown and the cheese golden, about 30 minutes. Remove the pizza from the oven and place on a wire rack to cool for 5 to 7 minutes.

If using a two-piece deep-dish pizza pan with removable sides, using long oven mitts, lift up the pizza pan. Center one hand underneath the bottom of the pan and slide the side ring of the pan off with the other hand. Carefully set the bottom of the pan back on the wire rack.

6   Cut the pizza into large wedges and serve immediately.

7   If using a one-piece deep-dish pizza pan, use a knife to loosen the crust from the sides of the pan. Cut the pizza into large wedges and then slide a metal spatula under the bottom crust to remove and lift out the wedges. Serve immediately.

Stuffed Pizza with Ricotta and Spinach

MAKES ONE 9-INCH STUFFED
PIZZA; SERVES 4 OR 5

OLIVE OIL FOR BRUSHING THE PAN

CHICAGO-STYLE DEEP-DISH PIZZA
DOUGH *(PAGE 68)* OR CHICAGO-
STYLE BUTTER-AND-GARLIC DEEP-
DISH PIZZA DOUGH *(PAGE 70)*, AT
ROOM TEMPERATURE

6 OUNCES BABY SPINACH LEAVES,
COARSELY CHOPPED

1 POUND WHOLE-MILK OR PART-
SKIM RICOTTA CHEESE

FRESHLY GROUND PEPPER

Stuffed pizzas are quite the sensation in Chicago. Different from deep-dish pizzas, these pizzas have both a bottom and top crust. There are so many good pizza joints in Chicago, it is difficult to mention them all; one we haven't talked about yet is Nancy's Original Stuffed Pizza. We ate this pizza many times at the original location on N. Elston Street on the upper northwest side of Chicago.

With some experimenting, we have adapted this recipe to perfection for the home cook. Not having the advantage of a commercial pizza oven, we found the best method for making a stuffed pizza was to cook it in a springform pan. Although an unconventional approach, releasing the clamp on the side of the pan partway through the baking process allows the steam to escape and the sides of the pizza to brown beautifully. This was a showstopper when we made it for a pizza party.

1 Position an oven rack on the second-lowest level in the oven and place a baking stone, if using one, on the rack. Preheat the oven to 450°F.

2 Brush the bottom and sides of a 9-inch round springform pan with olive oil. Remove one-quarter of the dough from the ball of prepared dough and set it aside, covered. Starting in the middle and using your fingertips, press the larger portion of dough evenly to cover the bottom and all the way up the sides of the pan, letting a bit of the dough overhang on the sides. Cover the pan with plastic wrap or a clean kitchen towel and let the dough rise in the pan for 10 minutes.

3 Meanwhile, combine the spinach and ricotta until well blended. Season with pepper.

4 To assemble the pizza, lightly press the dough up the sides of the pan if it has slid back down. Roll or press out the smaller piece of dough into a 9-inch circle and prick it all over with a fork. Lay half of the mozzarella slices over the pizza dough in the pan, overlapping them to cover the dough completely. Spoon the ricotta mixture over the top, spreading it evenly. Arrange the rest of the mozzarella over the top. Carefully fit the circle of dough over the cheese, and then fold down and roll the two edges of dough together to form a thick border.

8 OUNCES WHOLE-MILK OR
PART-SKIM, LOW-MOISTURE
MOZZARELLA, THINLY SLICED

2 CUPS SLOW-SIMMERED TOMATO
SAUCE (*PAGE 72*), AT ROOM
TEMPERATURE

¼ CUP (*1 OUNCE*) FRESHLY
GRATED PARMESAN CHEESE

5   Place the pizza in the oven on the rack or baking stone. (Work quickly to slide the pizza into the oven and close the door so the oven temperature doesn't drop too much.) Bake the pizza until the top crust is lightly browned, 12 minutes. Remove the pizza from the oven and ladle the tomato sauce evenly over the top crust without covering the edges. Sprinkle the Parmesan over the top of the sauce. Return the pizza to the oven and release the clamp on the side of the pan; this will allow the side crust to brown and crisp. Continue baking the pizza until the sides and top edges of the crust are deep golden brown, about 10 minutes longer. Using oven mitts, carefully relatch the clamp on the side of the pan, then remove the pizza from the oven and place it on a wire rack. Release the clamp and remove the side ring of the springform pan. Alternatively, without relatching the side ring, slide a pizza peel under both the bottom of the pan and the ring to transfer the pizza to a wire rack, then remove the ring. Let cool for 5 minutes.

6   Cut the pizza into large wedges and then slide a metal spatula under the bottom crust to remove and lift out the wedges. Serve immediately.

Deep-Dish Pizza with Zucchini, Onion, and Eggplant

MAKES ONE 14-INCH DEEP-DISH
PIZZA; SERVES 4 TO 6

2½ TABLESPOONS OLIVE OIL

CHICAGO-STYLE DEEP-DISH PIZZA
DOUGH (*PAGE 68*) OR CHICAGO-
STYLE BUTTER-AND-GARLIC DEEP-
DISH PIZZA DOUGH (*PAGE 70*), AT
ROOM TEMPERATURE

2 CLOVES GARLIC, MINCED

1 YELLOW ONION, CHOPPED

2 ZUCCHINI (*ABOUT 8 OUNCES
TOTAL*), CUT INTO ½-INCH DICE

1 EGGPLANT (*12 TO 14 OUNCES*),
CUT INTO ½-INCH DICE

1 TEASPOON KOSHER OR SEA SALT

FRESHLY GROUND PEPPER

This deep-dish pizza is a vegetarian delight, packed with chunks of onion, zucchini, and eggplant quickly sautéed in fruity olive oil until crisp-tender. A big hit of garlic punches up the Mediterranean vegetable combo. Oozing with cheese and topped with herb-infused tomato sauce, this is deep-dish pizza heaven, especially when made with the Chicago-Style Butter-and-Garlic Deep-Dish Pizza Dough.

1   Position an oven rack on the second-lowest level in the oven and place a baking stone, if using one, on the rack. Preheat the oven to 500°F.

2   Brush a 14-inch round deep-dish pizza pan with ½ tablespoon of the olive oil. Starting in the middle and using your fingertips, press the dough evenly to cover the bottom and about 2 inches up the sides of the pan. Cover the pan with plastic wrap or a clean kitchen towel and let the dough rise in the pan for 15 to 20 minutes.

3   Meanwhile, in a large skillet over medium-high heat, warm the remaining 2 tablespoons olive oil and swirl to coat the plan. Add the garlic and onion and sauté, stirring frequently, until soft but not brown, about 3 minutes. Add the zucchini and eggplant and continue to sauté until the vegetables are crisp-tender and beginning to brown at the edges, about 8 minutes longer. Season with the salt and pepper. Remove the pan from the heat and set aside to cool slightly.

4   To assemble the pizza, lightly press the dough up the sides of the pan if it has slid back down. Lay half of the mozzarella slices over the pizza dough, overlapping them to cover the dough completely. Scatter the cooked vegetables over the top. Arrange the rest of the mozzarella over the top. Ladle the tomato sauce evenly over the mozzarella. Sprinkle the Parmesan over the top of the sauce.

5   Place the pizza in the oven on the rack or baking stone and reduce the temperature to 450°F. (Work quickly to slide the pizza into the oven and close the door so the oven temperature doesn't drop too much.) Bake the pizza until the crust is crisp and a deep golden brown and the cheese is golden, about 30 minutes. Remove the pizza from the oven and place on a wire rack to cool for 5 to 7 minutes.

continued on next page ➙

1 POUND WHOLE-MILK OR
PART-SKIM, LOW-MOISTURE
MOZZARELLA, THINLY SLICED

3½ CUPS SLOW-SIMMERED
TOMATO SAUCE (*PAGE 72*), AT
ROOM TEMPERATURE

½ CUP (*2 OUNCES*) FRESHLY
GRATED PARMESAN CHEESE

6   If using a two-piece deep-dish pizza pan with removable sides, using long oven mitts, lift up the pizza pan. Center one hand underneath the bottom of the pan and slide the side ring of the pan off with the other hand. Carefully set the bottom of the pan back on the wire rack.

If using a one-piece deep-dish pizza pan, use a knife to loosen the crust from the sides of the pan.

7   Cut the pizza into large wedges and then slide a metal spatula under the bottom crust to remove and lift out the wedges. Serve immediately.

Deep-Dish Pizza with Spinach and Mozzarella

MAKES ONE 14-INCH DEEP-DISH
PIZZA; SERVES 4 TO 6

1½ TEASPOONS OLIVE OIL

CHICAGO-STYLE DEEP-DISH PIZZA
DOUGH *(PAGE 68)* OR CHICAGO-
STYLE BUTTER-AND-GARLIC DEEP-
DISH PIZZA DOUGH *(PAGE 70)*, AT
ROOM TEMPERATURE

1¼ POUNDS WHOLE-MILK OR
PART-SKIM, LOW-MOISTURE
MOZZARELLA, THINLY SLICED

10 OUNCES BABY SPINACH
LEAVES, COARSELY CHOPPED

1 TABLESPOON MINCED GARLIC

FRESHLY GROUND PEPPER

3½ CUPS SLOW-SIMMERED
TOMATO SAUCE *(PAGE 72)*, AT
ROOM TEMPERATURE

½ CUP *(2 OUNCES)* FRESHLY
GRATED PARMESAN CHEESE

As manly, beer-guzzling, and meaty a reputation as Chicago has, it may seem surprising that spinach pizzas are a huge hit on most pizzeria menus (Popeye would be proud!). Having tried this pizza with both cooked and uncooked spinach in the filling, the hands-down favorite was to use fresh spinach. Make sure you dry the spinach well before using. We prefer to buy the triple-washed baby spinach in plastic bags, because it saves time and the spinach is crisp and dry and has a small tender portion of the stem attached.

1   Position an oven rack on the second-lowest level in the oven and place a baking stone, if using one, on the rack. Preheat the oven to 500°F.

2   Brush a 14-inch round deep-dish pizza pan with the olive oil. Starting in the middle and using your fingertips, press the dough evenly to cover the bottom and about 2 inches up the sides of the pan. Cover the pan with plastic wrap or a clean kitchen towel and let the dough rise in the pan for 15 to 20 minutes.

3   To assemble the pizza, lightly press the dough up the sides of the pan if it has slid back down. Lay half of the mozzarella slices over the pizza dough, overlapping them to cover the dough completely. Toss the spinach with the garlic and a few grindings of pepper. Arrange the spinach mixture over the top of the mozzarella. Arrange the rest of the mozzarella over the spinach. Ladle the tomato sauce evenly over the mozzarella. Sprinkle the Parmesan over the top of the sauce.

4   Place the pizza in the oven on the rack or baking stone and reduce the temperature to 450°F. (Work quickly to slide the pizza into the oven and close the door so the oven temperature doesn't drop too much.) Bake the pizza until the crust is crisp and a deep golden brown and the cheese is golden, about 30 minutes. Remove the pizza from the oven and place on a wire rack to cool for 5 to 7 minutes.

5   If using a two-piece deep-dish pizza pan with removable sides, using long oven mitts, lift up the pizza pan. Center one hand underneath the bottom of the pan and slide the side ring of the pan off with the other hand. Carefully set the bottom of the pan back on the wire rack.

If using a one-piece deep-dish pizza pan, use a knife to loosen the crust from the sides of the pan.

6   Cut the pizza into large wedges and then slide a metal spatula under the bottom crust to remove and lift out the wedges. Serve immediately.

Deep-Dish Pizza with Green Peppers, Mushrooms, and Onions

MAKES ONE 14-INCH DEEP-DISH
PIZZA; SERVES 4 TO 6

1½ TEASPOONS OLIVE OIL

CHICAGO-STYLE DEEP-DISH PIZZA
DOUGH (PAGE 68) OR CHICAGO-
STYLE BUTTER-AND-GARLIC DEEP-
DISH PIZZA DOUGH (PAGE 70), AT
ROOM TEMPERATURE

1¼ POUNDS WHOLE-MILK OR
PART-SKIM, LOW-MOISTURE
MOZZARELLA, THINLY SLICED

½ WHITE ONION, CUT INTO
½-INCH DICE

1 GREEN BELL PEPPER, SEEDED,
DERIBBED, AND CUT INTO
½-INCH DICE

½ POUND BUTTON MUSHROOMS,
WIPED OR BRUSHED CLEAN,
SLICED ¼ INCH THICK

FRESHLY GROUND PEPPER

3½ CUPS SLOW-SIMMERED
TOMATO SAUCE (PAGE 72), AT
ROOM TEMPERATURE

½ CUP (2 OUNCES) FRESHLY
GRATED PARMESAN CHEESE

Here's another vegetarian-be-happy deep-dish pizza with a slightly more traditional filling. In this vegetable version, however, the onion, bell pepper, and mushrooms are layered without being cooked. With all the melted cheese under and over top, the veggies are crisp-tender and deliciously fresh tasting. You could use a sweet red bell pepper if you like; we prefer the assertive flavor of a green bell pepper.

1   Position an oven rack on the second-lowest level in the oven and place a baking stone, if using one, on the rack. Preheat the oven to 500°F.

2   Brush a 14-inch round deep-dish pizza pan with the olive oil. Starting in the middle and using your fingertips, press the dough evenly to cover the bottom and about 2 inches up the sides of the pan. Cover the pan with plastic wrap or a clean kitchen towel and let the dough rise in the pan for 15 to 20 minutes.

3   To assemble the pizza, lightly press the dough up the sides of the pan if it has slid back down. Lay half of the mozzarella slices over the pizza dough, overlapping them to cover the dough completely. Combine the onion and bell pepper and scatter over the mozzarella. Arrange the mushrooms over the top and season with a few grindings of pepper. Arrange the rest of the mozzarella over the mushrooms. Ladle the tomato sauce evenly over the mozzarella. Sprinkle the Parmesan over the top of the sauce.

4   Place the pizza in the oven on the rack or baking stone and reduce the temperature to 450°F. (Work quickly to slide the pizza into the oven and close the door so the oven temperature doesn't drop too much.) Bake the pizza until the crust is crisp and a deep golden brown and the cheese is golden, about 30 minutes. Remove the pizza from the oven and place on a wire rack to cool for 5 to 7 minutes.

5   If using a two-piece deep-dish pizza pan with removable sides, using long oven mitts, lift up the pizza pan. Center one hand underneath the bottom of the pan and slide the side ring of the pan off with the other hand. Carefully set the bottom of the pan back on the wire rack.

If using a one-piece deep-dish pizza pan, use a knife to loosen the crust from the sides of the pan.

6   Cut the pizza into large wedges and then slide a metal spatula under the bottom crust to remove and lift out the wedges. Serve immediately.

Edwardo's Famous Stuffed Spinach Pizza

MAKES ONE 9-INCH STUFFED
PIZZA; SERVES 4 OR 5

OLIVE OIL FOR BRUSHING THE PAN

CHICAGO-STYLE DEEP-DISH PIZZA
DOUGH *(PAGE 68)*, AT ROOM
TEMPERATURE

8 OUNCES BABY SPINACH LEAVES,
COARSELY CHOPPED

2 CUPS *(8 OUNCES)* COARSELY
SHREDDED WHOLE-MILK OR
PART-SKIM, LOW-MOISTURE
MOZZARELLA CHEESE, PLUS
3 OUNCES, THINLY SLICED

FRESHLY GROUND PEPPER

2 CUPS SLOW-SIMMERED TOMATO
SAUCE *(PAGE 72)*, AT ROOM
TEMPERATURE

⅓ CUP *(1½ OUNCES)* FRESHLY
GRATED PARMESAN CHEESE

Edwardo's was a late bloomer on the Chicago pizza scene—but what a sensation when it opened, in 1978! The pizzeria became famous almost immediately for its "Spinach Soufflé Pizza." If you've never tried it, you are probably imagining something like Stouffer's frozen spinach soufflé stuffed inside a crust. It's not even close. Fresh, coarsely chopped spinach is tossed with loads of shredded mozzarella and a generous grinding of black pepper. A layer of sliced mozzarella is tiled over the bottom dough to keep it from getting soggy. The spinach and cheese mixture is mounded in and then covered with a top of dough. The pizza is baked to allow the crust to set and puff before being topped with tomato sauce and Parmesan. This is an amazing stuffed pizza.

1   Position an oven rack on the second-lowest level in the oven and place a baking stone, if using one, on the rack. Preheat the oven to 450°F.

2   Brush the bottom and sides of a 9-inch round springform pan with olive oil. Remove one-quarter of the dough from the ball of prepared dough and set it aside, covered. Starting in the middle and using your hands, press and stretch the dough evenly to cover the bottom and all the way up the sides of the pan, letting a bit of the dough overhang on the sides. Cover the pan with plastic wrap or a clean kitchen towel and let the dough rise in the pan for 10 minutes.

3   Meanwhile, toss together the spinach and shredded mozzarella until well blended. Season with pepper.

4   To assemble the pizza, lightly press the dough up the sides of the pan if it has slid back down. Roll or press out the smaller piece of dough into a 9-inch circle and prick it all over with a fork. Lay the mozzarella slices over the pizza dough in the pan, overlapping them to cover the dough completely. Spread the spinach mixture evenly over the sliced cheese. Carefully fit the circle of dough over the spinach mixture, and then fold down and roll the two edges of dough together to form a thick border.

continued on page 85 ➜

5   Place the pizza in the oven on the rack or baking stone. (Work quickly to slide the pizza into the oven and close the door so the oven temperature doesn't drop too much.) Bake the pizza until the top crust is lightly browned, 12 minutes. Remove the pizza from the oven and ladle the tomato sauce evenly over the top crust without covering the edges. Sprinkle the Parmesan over the top of the sauce. Return the pizza to the oven and release the clamp on the side of the pan; this will allow the side crust to brown and crisp. Continue to bake the pizza until the sides and top edges of the crust are deep golden brown, about 10 minutes longer. Using oven mitts, carefully relatch the clamp on the side of the pan, then remove the pizza from the oven and place it on a wire rack. Release the clamp and remove the side ring of the springform pan. Alternatively, without relatching the side ring, slide a pizza peel under both the bottom of the pan and the ring to transfer the pizza to a wire rack, then remove the ring. Let cool for 5 minutes.

6   Cut the pizza into large wedges and then slide a metal spatula under the bottom crust to remove and lift out the wedges. Serve immediately.

CHAPTER

5

California-Style Pizza

By the time Tony shook the principal's hand and received his high-school diploma, his older brother Frank, then twenty-two, had talked Tony into opening a pizzeria with him. Frank had worked in a couple of pizzerias and learned the business, but both were naturals in the kitchen, having watched and learned from their mother. Pyzano's opened in 1991 in Castro Valley, California. When asked about the name, Tony tells the story of his grandfather never being able to keep their friends' names straight. His grandfather's solution was to call all their friends "paisano." So, Frank decided to Americanize the Spanish word, and named the pizzeria Pyzano's.

Frank created the first eight pizzas on the menu and taught Tony how to throw a pizza. Always ready to party and have fun, Tony decided to throw pizzas in view in the restaurant as a way to entertain the kids and their families coming to dine. A few tricks later, being able to toss and spin pizzas at dizzying speeds, Tony entered the World Pizza Games in Las Vegas in 1995. He competed in the freestyle acrobatic pizza tossing competition and won first place. He won again in 1996 and 1997, adding a few new tricks each year. At this point, Tony could spin and toss pizzas between his legs while lying on his back and scissor-kicking; he could also roll two wheels of dough on their edges in opposite directions along the length of each arm. (The latter trick became known around the world as "the Gemignani.") He even did tricks blindfolded.

Tony went to Italy in 2000 to compete with the big boys in the World Pizza Championships. This time, Tony faced sixty pizza acrobats, many of whom had trained at Italian pizza-tossing schools. He tied for first place in 2000 and won in 2001. After winning back-to-back competitions, Tony was asked to stop competing and start judging, a great honor. He was then asked to coach the U.S. Pizza Team, which he did in 2002, 2003, and 2004. Tony has since created instructional DVDs and trade-marked a synthetic practice dough that glows in the dark (see Sources, page 160).

While traveling and training pizza makers and chefs all around the world, Tony learned different styles of pizza making and so started to incorporate international flavors into his pizzas at Pyzano's. California-style pizza making has always taken a liberal interpretation of what defines pizza, topping pizzas with nontraditional cheeses, nontypical meats like duck and chicken, and even throwing on some fruit if the mood struck. Cross-cultural influences are strong in California, so why not encompass that in pizza making? This chapter will most likely expand your horizons as to what a pizza can be. Tony made a dazzling selection of pizzas for Diane when she visited Pyzano's for the first time, and she was overwhelmed and amazed (stuffed, too). They're all here—straight from the champ and the pizzeria that has been ranked one of the top ten pizza destinations in the United States.

Tony's Pizza Dough

MAKES 44 OUNCES DOUGH,
ENOUGH FOR TWO
14-INCH PIZZAS

1 PACKAGE (2¼ TEASPOONS)
ACTIVE DRY YEAST

1 CUP LUKEWARM WATER
(90° TO 100°F)

1 CUP ICE-COLD WATER

1 TABLESPOON SUGAR

1 TABLESPOON TABLE SALT OR
1½ TABLESPOONS KOSHER SALT

2 TABLESPOONS OLIVE OIL

5¼ TO 5½ CUPS UNBLEACHED
BREAD FLOUR, PLUS MORE FOR
DUSTING (SEE COOK'S NOTE)

At Pyzano's, they use 32 pounds of flour per batch of dough, and they make nine to fourteen batches a day. We've cut the recipe down for the home cook. This recipe makes enough dough for two pizzas. This dough is not too soft or sticky, making it perfect for tossing and throwing. It is also a very manageable dough for the novice pizza maker. Plan ahead when making these pizzas, because Tony uses a cold rise method for his dough. Once the dough is made, it is portioned and placed in the refrigerator to rise slowly for at least 10 hours. The advantage here is that the dough can be made the day or evening before a party, or even early in the morning on the day you plan to use it. With a little organization—say, making dough on Sunday for a Monday night dinner—homemade pizza as a weeknight meal is a real possibility.

1   In a small bowl, using a fork, stir the yeast into the lukewarm water. Set aside until the yeast dissolves, about 5 minutes.

2   In another small bowl, combine the cold water, sugar, salt, and olive oil. Stir to dissolve the sugar and salt.

3   To make the dough by hand: Place 5¼ cups of the flour in a large bowl. Make a well in the center of the flour and stir in the yeast mixture along with the cold-water mixture. Using a wooden spoon, mix the dough, incorporating as much of the flour as possible. Turn the dough out on a lightly floured work surface and knead until soft and elastic, 10 to 12 minutes. It will still be a little sticky but shouldn't stick to your hands. Add only a minimum amount of flour to the work surface to keep the dough from sticking.

To make the dough using a mixer: Fit a heavy-duty stand mixer with the dough hook attachment. Place 5¼ cups of the flour in the mixer bowl. Add the yeast mixture along with the cold-water mixture and mix on low speed until the flour is incorporated and the dough gathers together to form a coarse ball, about 4 minutes. Let rest for 2 minutes, then mix on low speed until the dough is smooth and not sticky, about 6 minutes longer. (If the dough begins to climb up the dough hook toward the motor drive, stop the mixer and push it down. If the machine labors and the motor feels hot, stop and wait a few minutes for the motor to cool down.) Turn the dough out on a well-floured work surface and knead for a minute or two until it forms a smooth ball, adding up to ¼ cup of additional flour, if necessary.

4   Cut the dough in half to form two even portions, each weighing 22 ounces. With floured hands, pick up one portion of dough and pull the opposite edges together, wrapping them underneath toward the center to form a tight smooth ball. Pinch to seal. Repeat with the second portion. Place each portion in a 1-gallon lock-top plastic bag. Squeeze out all the air and seal the bags, allowing enough room for the dough to double in size.

5   Refrigerate for at least 10 hours or up to 2 days. Remove from the refrigerator 1 hour before using to allow the dough to come to room temperature. Proceed with any California-style pizza recipe.

COOK'S NOTE

This dough recipe works best with unbleached bread flour with at least 12.5 percent protein. Although commercial bakers and pizza makers can buy unbleached bread flour that is 13.5 percent protein (that's what Tony uses), it isn't readily available at retail. However, we had great results using King Arthur's unbleached bread flour with 12.7 percent protein.

Tony's Pizza Sauce

MAKES 3½ CUPS

4 CANS (6 OUNCES EACH) TOMATO PASTE

¾ CUP WATER

1½ TABLESPOONS EXTRA-VIRGIN OLIVE OIL

2 TABLESPOONS SUGAR

1½ TABLESPOONS TABLE SALT OR 2½ TABLESPOONS KOSHER SALT

1 TABLESPOON PLUS 1 TEASPOON DRIED OREGANO

1 TEASPOON DRIED BASIL

¼ TEASPOON GARLIC POWDER

4 LARGE FRESH BASIL LEAVES, CHOPPED

Tony refers to this as his "super-heavy" pizza sauce. It is a robust sauce that holds up well and will never make a pizza crust soggy. Cut the recipe in half if you are making only a couple of pizzas, or freeze the leftovers in small quantities for future pizza making.

In a large bowl, using a wire whisk, combine the tomato paste, water, and olive oil. Add the sugar, salt, oregano, dried basil, and garlic powder and whisk until well combined. Stir in the fresh basil. Use immediately, or store in a tightly covered container in the refrigerator for up to 5 days, or freeze for up to 2 months. Bring to room temperature before using.

Barbecued Chicken, Cheddar, Onion, Bell Pepper, and BBQ Sauce Pizza

MAKES ONE 14-INCH PIZZA;
SERVES 4 TO 6

2 CUPS SHREDDED SAUTÉED OR ROAST CHICKEN BREAST

¾ CUP BOTTLED BARBECUE SAUCE

VEGETABLE-OIL COOKING SPRAY

1 PORTION (22 OUNCES) TONY'S PIZZA DOUGH (PAGE 88), AT ROOM TEMPERATURE

UNBLEACHED BREAD FLOUR FOR DUSTING

¾ CUP THINLY SLICED WHITE ONION

1 TABLESPOON MINCED GARLIC

1 RED BELL PEPPER, HALVED LENGTHWISE, SEEDED, DERIBBED, AND CUT INTO THIN STRIPS

2 CUPS (8 OUNCES) COARSELY SHREDDED MEDIUM OR SHARP CHEDDAR CHEESE

¼ CUP LIGHTLY PACKED FRESH CILANTRO LEAVES

Everyone likes anything barbecue, so why not put it on pizza? Use leftover chicken, or buy a rotisserie chicken and shred the breast meat. We don't specify a particular barbecue sauce; use your favorite version, though one with a kick of heat makes the pizza terrific. Diane's family is partial to Bryant's barbecue sauce, because her husband grew up in Kansas City (see Sources, page 160).

1   Position an oven rack on the second-lowest level in the oven and place a baking stone on the rack. Position another rack in the upper third of the oven. Preheat the oven to 500°F.

2   While the oven is heating, prepare the toppings: In a medium bowl, toss the shredded chicken with ¼ cup of barbecue sauce. Set aside. Have all the other ingredients measured, chopped, and ready for assembly.

3   Coat a 14-inch pizza screen or perforated pizza pan with the cooking spray. Remove the dough from the plastic bag and place on a lightly floured work surface. Lightly dust the dough with flour. Using a rolling pin, roll the dough into a 10-inch round without rolling over the edges. Lift the dough and check to make sure the dough isn't sticking to the work surface. Shake the excess flour from the dough. Following the Dough-Tossing Techniques on page 22, toss the dough until it is stretched to a 14-inch circle and place it on the prepared pizza screen or pan. Alternatively, lay the dough on the prepared screen or pan and gently stretch the dough into a 14-inch round.

4   To top the pizza: Spread the remaining ½ cup barbecue sauce over the dough, leaving a 1-inch border. Evenly scatter the onion, garlic, and bell pepper over the sauce. Distribute the chicken evenly over the vegetables. Top with the cheese.

5   Place the pizza in the oven on the upper rack. (Work quickly to slide the pizza into the oven and close the door so the oven temperature doesn't drop too much.) Bake the pizza until the crust is crisp and golden brown, 8 to 10 minutes. Using a pizza peel, lift the pizza off the screen or pan and place the crust directly on the baking stone. Using the peel or wearing thick oven mitts, remove the screen or pan from the oven. Bake the pizza until the bottom of the crust is golden brown, 3 to 4 minutes longer. Using the peel, remove the pizza from the oven and transfer to a cutting board. Scatter the cilantro over the top. Slice the pizza into wedges and serve immediately.

Tony's Famous Cholula Spicy Chicken Pizza

MAKES ONE 14-INCH PIZZA;
SERVES 4 TO 6

1½ CUPS SHREDDED SAUTÉED OR ROAST CHICKEN BREAST

¼ CUP BOTTLED CHOLULA OR OTHER HOT SAUCE

VEGETABLE-OIL COOKING SPRAY

1 PORTION (22 OUNCES) TONY'S PIZZA DOUGH (PAGE 88), AT ROOM TEMPERATURE

UNBLEACHED BREAD FLOUR FOR DUSTING

¾ CUP TONY'S PIZZA SAUCE (PAGE 90)

2 CUPS (8 OUNCES) COARSELY SHREDDED WHOLE-MILK OR PART-SKIM, LOW-MOISTURE MOZZARELLA CHEESE

Tony developed this pizza because his Korean pizza delivery driver, Daniel Lee, kept insisting that none of his pizzas were spicy enough. As a prank, Tony made an extra-large pizza with about 2 ounces of diced habenero peppers hidden under the cheese. Tony served it to Daniel and waited and watched. Seconds later, sweat was pouring down Daniel's brow, tears were running down his cheeks. Daniel waved and exclaimed, "You got it, you got it!" From this early experiment the Cholula pizza was born. Tony uses jalapeños instead of habeneros to tame the heat for most customers. Rev up the spice quotient, if you like. This pizza is an all-time favorite at the restaurant.

1   Position an oven rack on the second-lowest level in the oven and place a baking stone on the rack. Position another rack in the upper third of the oven. Preheat the oven to 500°F.

2   While the oven is heating, toss the shredded chicken with the hot sauce. Set aside. Have all the other ingredients measured, chopped, and ready for assembly.

3   Coat a 14-inch pizza screen or perforated pizza pan with the cooking spray. Remove the dough from the plastic bag and place on a lightly floured work surface. Lightly dust the dough with flour. Using a rolling pin, roll the dough into a 10-inch round without rolling over the edges. Lift the dough and check to make sure the dough isn't sticking to the work surface. Shake the excess flour from the dough. Following the Dough-Tossing Techniques on page 22, toss the dough until it is stretched to a 14-inch circle and place it on the prepared pizza screen or pan. Alternatively, lay the dough on the prepared screen or pan and gently stretch the dough into a 14-inch round.

4   To top the pizza: Spread the pizza sauce over the dough, leaving a 1-inch border. Arrange the chicken evenly over the sauce. Scatter the mozzarella over the top. Evenly distribute the onion, jalapeño, garlic, and chorizo over the cheese.

continued on next page

¾ CUP THINLY SLICED RED ONION

1 OR 2 JALAPEÑO CHILES,
INCLUDING SEEDS, THINLY SLICED
INTO ROUNDS

1 TABLESPOON MINCED GARLIC

4 OUNCES UNCOOKED CHORIZO,
CUT INTO ½-INCH CHUNKS

PAPRIKA FOR DUSTING

5   Place the pizza in the oven on the upper rack. (Work quickly to slide the pizza into the oven and close the door so the oven temperature doesn't drop too much.) Bake the pizza until the crust is crisp and golden brown, 8 to 10 minutes. Using a pizza peel, lift the pizza off the screen or pan and place the crust directly on the baking stone. Using the peel or wearing thick oven mitts, remove the screen or pan from the oven. Bake the pizza until the bottom of the crust is golden brown, 3 to 4 minutes longer. Using the peel, remove the pizza from the oven and transfer to a cutting board. Dust the pizza very lightly with paprika. Slice the pizza into wedges and serve immediately.

Tony's Favorite Vegetable Pizza

MAKES ONE 14-INCH PIZZA;
SERVES 4 TO 6

When Tony was asked to appear on the television show *Bay Café*, with host Joey Altman, the producers wanted Tony to make a vegetarian pizza. The pie he came up with was a huge hit on the show. Customers at his restaurant, having seen the show, kept asking for the pizza, even though it wasn't on the menu at the time. Every time they rerun the show, Pyzano's get packed, and everyone is ordering the "TV" vegetarian pizza. This is a winning combo.

VEGETABLE-OIL COOKING SPRAY

1 PORTION *(22 OUNCES)* TONY'S PIZZA DOUGH *(PAGE 88)*, AT ROOM TEMPERATURE

UNBLEACHED BREAD FLOUR FOR DUSTING

1 CUP TONY'S PIZZA SAUCE *(PAGE 90)*

½ CUP DRAINED SUN-DRIED TOMATOES

1 SMALL ZUCCHINI, CUT INTO THIN ROUNDS

2 CUPS *(8 OUNCES)* COARSELY SHREDDED WHOLE-MILK OR PART-SKIM, LOW-MOISTURE MOZZARELLA CHEESE

½ CUP THINLY SLICED RED ONION

1 GREEN BELL PEPPER, CUT CROSSWISE INTO THIN ROUNDS, CORE, SEEDS, AND RIBS REMOVED

1 JAR *(6½ OUNCES)* MARINATED ARTICHOKE HEARTS, DRAINED

1   Position an oven rack on the second-lowest level in the oven and place a baking stone on the rack. Position another rack in the upper third of the oven. Preheat the oven to 500°F.

2   Coat a 14-inch pizza screen or perforated pizza pan with the cooking spray. Remove the dough from the plastic bag and place on a lightly floured work surface. Lightly dust the dough with flour. Using a rolling pin, roll the dough into a 10-inch round without rolling over the edges. Lift the dough and check to make sure the dough isn't sticking to the work surface. Shake the excess flour from the dough. Following the Dough-Tossing Techniques on page 22, toss the dough until it is stretched to a 14-inch circle and place it on the prepared pizza screen or pan. Alternatively, lay the dough on the prepared screen or pan and gently stretch the dough into a 14-inch round.

3   To top the pizza: Spread the pizza sauce over the dough, leaving a 1-inch border. Arrange the tomatoes and zucchini evenly over the sauce. Scatter the mozzarella over the top. Evenly distribute the red onion, bell pepper, and artichoke hearts over the cheese.

4   Place the pizza in the oven on the upper rack. (Work quickly to slide the pizza into the oven and close the door so the oven temperature doesn't drop too much.) Bake the pizza until the crust is crisp and golden brown, 8 to 10 minutes. Using a pizza peel, lift the pizza off the screen or pan and place the crust directly on the baking stone. Using the peel or wearing thick oven mitts, remove the screen or pan from the oven. Bake the pizza until the bottom of the crust is golden brown, 3 to 4 minutes longer. Using the peel, remove the pizza from the oven and transfer to a cutting board. Slice the pizza into wedges and serve immediately.

West Coast White Pizza

MAKES ONE 14-INCH PIZZA;
SERVES 4 TO 6

1½ CUPS SHREDDED SAUTÉED OR ROAST CHICKEN BREAST

¼ CUP, PLUS ⅓ CUP BOTTLED RANCH DRESSING

VEGETABLE-OIL COOKING SPRAY

1 PORTION (22 OUNCES) TONY'S PIZZA DOUGH (PAGE 88), AT ROOM TEMPERATURE

UNBLEACHED BREAD FLOUR FOR DUSTING

1 TABLESPOON MINCED GARLIC

½ CUP (2 OUNCES) COARSELY SHREDDED PROVOLONE CHEESE

1½ CUPS (6 OUNCES) COARSELY SHREDDED WHOLE-MILK OR PART-SKIM, LOW-MOISTURE MOZZARELLA CHEESE

Over the years at Pyzano's, chicken has replaced sausage and pepperoni as the meat topping of choice. Furthermore, customers would often order a pizza with chicken and then order ranch dressing on the side. Because of this, experimenting one day, as Tony often does, he decided to toss some cooked chicken with ranch dressing, spread a little ranch dressing on the dough instead of tomato sauce, and top the pizza with a mixture of cheeses. The resulting pizza was well received, and the "West Coast White Pizza" was born. Of all the California pizzas Tony proposed for inclusion in this book, this was the one that Diane was most skeptical of liking because she isn't a fan of ranch dressing. As she found out, though, you don't have to like ranch dressing to love this pizza—it's incredible.

1   Position an oven rack on the second-lowest level in the oven and place a baking stone on the rack. Position another rack in the upper third of the oven. Preheat the oven to 500°F.

2   While the oven is heating, toss the shredded chicken with ¼ cup of the ranch dressing. Set aside. Have all the other ingredients measured, chopped, and ready for assembly.

3   Coat a 14-inch pizza screen or perforated pizza pan with the cooking spray. Remove the dough from the plastic bag and place on a lightly floured work surface. Lightly dust the dough with flour. Using a rolling pin, roll the dough into a 10-inch round without rolling over the edges. Lift the dough and check to make sure the dough isn't sticking to the work surface. Shake the excess flour from the dough. Following the Dough-Tossing Techniques on page 22, toss the dough until it is stretched to a 14-inch circle and place it on the prepared pizza screen or pan. Alternatively, lay the dough on the prepared screen or pan and gently stretch the dough into a 14-inch round.

1/3 CUP (ABOUT 2 OUNCES) WHOLE-MILK RICOTTA CHEESE

1/2 TEASPOON DRIED THYME

1 LARGE ROMA TOMATO, THINLY SLICED

4   To top the pizza: Spread the remaining 1/3 cup ranch dressing over the dough, leaving a 1-inch border. Arrange the chicken evenly over the sauce. Evenly distribute the garlic over the chicken. Scatter the provolone and mozzarella cheeses over the top. Evenly distribute little globs of ricotta over the other cheeses. Crush the thyme between your fingers and sprinkle it evenly over the cheeses.

5   Place the pizza in the oven on the upper rack. (Work quickly to slide the pizza into the oven and close the door so the oven temperature doesn't drop too much.) Bake the pizza until the crust is crisp and golden brown, 10 minutes. Using a pizza peel, lift the pizza off the screen or pan and place the crust directly on the baking stone. Using the peel or wearing thick oven mitts, remove the screen or pan from the oven. Bake the pizza until the bottom of the crust is golden brown, about 3 minutes longer. Using the peel, remove the pizza from the oven and transfer to a cutting board. Slice the pizza into wedges, place a slice of tomato on each wedge, and serve immediately.

Thai Curry Chicken Pizza

MAKES ONE 14-INCH PIZZA; SERVES 4 TO 6

2 TEASPOONS VEGETABLE OIL

1½ TABLESPOONS THAI GREEN CURRY PASTE (SEE COOK'S NOTE)

1 CAN (13.5 OUNCES) UNSWEETENED COCONUT MILK

2 TABLESPOONS THAI FISH SAUCE (NAM PLA)

2 TABLESPOONS PACKED DARK BROWN SUGAR

1½ TEASPOONS FRESH LIME JUICE

1 WHOLE BONELESS, SKINLESS CHICKEN BREAST (ABOUT 14 OUNCES), CUT CROSSWISE INTO THIN STRIPS

⅓ CUP COARSELY CHOPPED FRESH BASIL LEAVES, PLUS 3 LARGE LEAVES CUT CROSSWISE INTO THIN RIBBONS FOR GARNISH

¼ CUP DICED CANNED BAMBOO SHOOTS

In 1997, Tony did a traveling pizza show in Thailand. He met Supakit Rungrote, who owns about ten New York–style pizza franchises in Bangkok. Tony bonded with him, both being acrobatic pizza throwers, and they traveled together for a time. Supakit introduced Tony to lots of Thai food, including an especially memorable Thai curry chicken dish. When Tony got home, he decided to develop a curry chicken pizza in Supakit's honor. This is the pizza—exotic, spicy, and delicious.

1   Position an oven rack on the second-lowest level in the oven and place a baking stone on the rack. Position another rack in the upper third of the oven. Preheat the oven to 500°F.

2   While the oven is heating, prepare the toppings: In a medium saucepan, warm the oil over low heat and stir in the curry paste. Add the coconut milk, fish sauce, brown sugar, and lime juice. Raise the heat to medium and bring to a simmer. Add the chicken, chopped basil, and bamboo shoots and simmer until the chicken is cooked through, about 10 minutes. Using a slotted spoon, drain the chicken and bamboo shoots and transfer to a plate to cool. Raise the heat to medium high and boil the sauce until it is reduced to about ⅔ cup. Set aside to cool.

3   Coat a 14-inch pizza screen or perforated pizza pan with the cooking spray. Remove the dough from the plastic bag and place on a lightly floured work surface. Lightly dust the dough with flour. Using a rolling pin, roll the dough into a 10-inch round without rolling over the edges. Lift the dough and check to make sure the dough isn't sticking to the work surface. Shake the excess flour from the dough. Following the Dough-Tossing Techniques on page 22, toss the dough until it is stretched to a 14-inch circle and place it on the prepared pizza screen or pan. Alternatively, lay the dough on the prepared screen or pan and gently stretch the dough into a 14-inch round.

continued on next page →

VEGETABLE-OIL COOKING SPRAY

1 PORTION *(22 OUNCES)* TONY'S
PIZZA DOUGH *(PAGE 88)*, AT
ROOM TEMPERATURE

UNBLEACHED BREAD FLOUR FOR
DUSTING

2 CUPS *(8 OUNCES)* COARSELY
SHREDDED WHOLE-MILK OR
PART-SKIM, LOW-MOISTURE
MOZZARELLA CHEESE

½ RED BELL PEPPER, SEEDED,
DERIBBED, AND JULIENNED

⅓ CUP PEELED AND COARSELY
GRATED CARROT

4   To top the pizza: Spread the reduced sauce over the dough, leaving a 1-inch border. Drain and discard any juice from the chicken and bamboo shoots and arrange in a single layer over the sauce. Evenly distribute the mozzarella over the top.

5   Place the pizza in the oven on the upper rack. (Work quickly to slide the pizza into the oven and close the door so the oven temperature doesn't drop too much.) Bake the pizza until the crust is crisp and golden brown, 10 minutes. Using a pizza peel, lift the pizza off the screen or pan and place the crust directly on the baking stone. Using the peel or wearing thick oven mitts, remove the screen or pan from the oven. Bake the pizza until the bottom of the crust is golden brown, about 3 minutes longer. Using the peel, remove the pizza from the oven and transfer to a cutting board. Scatter the bell pepper, carrot, and basil ribbons over the pizza. Slice the pizza into wedges and serve immediately.

COOK'S NOTE

Thai green curry paste is available in small jars or cans at supermarkets or Asian grocery stores. Green curry paste is made of green chiles, lemongrass, garlic, galangal, kaffir lime peel, and spices. It is moderately spicy. Use more or less to please your taste buds.

Big Kahuna Pizza

MAKES ONE 14-INCH PIZZA;
SERVES 4 TO 6

1½ TABLESPOONS OLIVE OIL

1 TABLESPOON MINCED GARLIC

6 LARGE SHRIMP, PEELED AND
DEVEINED

6 THIN SLICES *(ABOUT 3 OUNCES)*
PROSCIUTTO DI PARMA

¼ CUP ANGEL FLAKE COCONUT

VEGETABLE-OIL COOKING SPRAY

1 PORTION *(22 OUNCES)* TONY'S
PIZZA DOUGH *(PAGE 88)*, AT
ROOM TEMPERATURE

UNBLEACHED BREAD FLOUR FOR
DUSTING

Just as a rivalry exists between New York and Chicago as to what constitutes pizza, a rivalry exists between New York pizza makers and those making California-style pizza. The New York guys are always razzing Tony, saying, "How's that pineapple pizza doing in California?" Instead of chafing at the heat, Tony turned his energy and creativity to making a fabulous pineapple pizza, with the addition of shrimp and prosciutto. Making a nod to Hawaiian flavors, Tony lays pineapple slices over shredded mozzarella and then arranges slices of prosciutto with whole shrimp and coconut rolled up inside among the pineapple slices. Coconut is scattered over the top after the pizza is baked, and maraschino cherries colorfully dot the pie. This is a true California pizza delight.

1   Position an oven rack on the second-lowest level in the oven and place a baking stone on the rack. Position another rack in the upper third of the oven. Preheat the oven to 500°F.

2   While the oven is heating, prepare the top-pings: In a small skillet, preferably nonstick, warm the olive oil over medium heat and swirl to coat the pan. Add half of the garlic and sauté, stirring constantly, until just beginning to color, about 30 seconds. Add the shrimp and sauté just until the shrimp turn pink, about 3 minutes. Set aside to cool. Separate the slices of prosciutto and arrange on a work surface. Place a cooled shrimp at one end of each slice. Sprinkle a teaspoon of coconut over each shrimp. Tightly roll each slice in a cylinder, with the shrimp in the center. Set aside. Have all the other ingredients measured, shredded, and ready for assembly.

3   Coat a 14-inch pizza screen or perforated pizza pan with the cooking spray. Remove the dough from the plastic bag and place on a lightly floured work surface. Lightly dust the dough with flour. Using a rolling pin, roll the dough into a 10-inch round without rolling over the edges. Lift the dough and check to make sure the dough isn't sticking to the work surface. Shake the excess flour from the dough. Following the Dough-Tossing Techniques on page 22, toss the dough until it is stretched to a 14-inch circle and place it on the prepared pizza screen orpan. Alternatively, lay the dough on the prepared screen or pan and gently stretch the dough into a 14-inch round.

continued on next page →

Big Kahuna Pizza *continued*

¾ CUP TONY'S PIZZA SAUCE
(PAGE 90)

2 CUPS (8 OUNCES) COARSELY
SHREDDED WHOLE-MILK OR
PART-SKIM, LOW-MOISTURE
MOZZARELLA CHEESE

7 SLICES CANNED UNSWEETENED
PINEAPPLE, WELL DRAINED

7 MARASCHINO CHERRIES, WELL
DRAINED AND STEMS REMOVED

4   To top the pizza: Spread the pizza sauce over the dough, leaving a 1-inch border. Sprinkle the remaining garlic over the sauce. Scatter the mozzarella evenly over the sauce. Place a slice of pineapple in the center of the pizza. Alternate slices of pineapple with the shrimp-wrapped prosciutto and place them around the edge of the pizza, retaining the 1-inch border. Place a cherry in the center of each slice of pineapple.

5   Place the pizza in the oven on the upper rack. (Work quickly to slide the pizza into the oven and close the door so the oven temperature doesn't drop too much.) Bake the pizza until the crust is crisp and golden brown, 8 to 10 minutes. Using a pizza peel, lift the pizza off the screen or pan and place the crust directly on the baking stone. Using the peel or wearing thick oven mitts, remove the screen or pan from the oven. Bake the pizza until the bottom of the crust is golden brown, 3 to 4 minutes longer. Using the peel, remove the pizza from the oven and transfer to a cutting board. Sprinkle the remaining coconut over the pizza. Slice the pizza into wedges and serve immediately.

Chicken Caesar Salad Pizza

MAKES ONE 14-INCH PIZZA;
SERVES 4 TO 6

1½ CUPS SHREDDED SAUTÉED OR
ROAST CHICKEN BREAST

½ CUP BOTTLED CREAMY CAESAR
DRESSING (*SEE COOK'S NOTE,
PAGE 104*)

2 TEASPOONS MINCED GARLIC

VEGETABLE-OIL COOKING SPRAY

1 PORTION (*22 OUNCES*) TONY'S
PIZZA DOUGH (*PAGE 88*), AT
ROOM TEMPERATURE

UNBLEACHED BREAD FLOUR FOR
DUSTING

½ CUP (*2 OUNCES*) COARSELY
SHREDDED PROVOLONE CHEESE

1⅔ CUPS (*7 OUNCES*) COARSELY
SHREDDED WHOLE-MILK OR
PART-SKIM, LOW-MOISTURE
MOZZARELLA CHEESE

In the '90s, after breaking up with his girlfriend, Tony decided to get into shape. He went to the gym five times a week and ate chicken Caesar salads every day instead of pizza. One day, thinking about the pizza special for the coming week, Tony decided to experiment and make a chicken Caesar salad pizza. Tony tossed shredded cooked chicken with Caesar dressing, spread some Caesar dressing on the dough, layered on garlic, chicken, and cheese, and baked it. He scattered ribbons of romaine lettuce over top, placed tomato slices around the edges, and scattered coarsely shaved Parmesan over the top. It's a Caesar! Asked about croutons, Tony says, "Consider the pizza crust to be one big crouton."

1   Position an oven rack on the second-lowest level in the oven and place a baking stone on the rack. Position another rack in the upper third of the oven. Preheat the oven to 500°F.

2   While the oven is heating, toss the shredded chicken with ¼ cup of the Caesar dressing and the garlic. Set aside. Have all the other ingredients measured, sliced, and ready for assembly.

3   Coat a 14-inch pizza screen or perforated pizza pan with the cooking spray. Remove the dough from the plastic bag and place on a lightly floured work surface. Lightly dust the dough with flour. Using a rolling pin, roll the dough into a 10-inch round without rolling over the edges. Lift the dough and check to make sure the dough isn't sticking to the work surface. Shake the excess flour from the dough. Following the Dough-Tossing Techniques on page 22, toss the dough until it is stretched to a 14-inch circle and place it on the prepared pizza screen or pan. Alternatively, lay the dough on the prepared screen or pan and gently stretch the dough into a 14-inch round.

4   To top the pizza: Spread the remaining ¼ cup of Caesar dressing over the dough, leaving a 1-inch border. Arrange the chicken mixture evenly over the sauce. Scatter the provolone and mozzarella cheeses over the top.

continued on next page →

2 LARGE LEAVES ROMAINE
LETTUCE, HALVED LENGTHWISE
AND SLICED CROSSWISE INTO
THIN RIBBONS

1 LARGE ROMA TOMATO, THINLY
SLICED

3 TABLESPOONS COARSELY SHAVED
PARMESAN CHEESE, PREFERABLY
PARMIGIANO-REGGIANO

5   Place the pizza in the oven on the upper rack. (Work quickly to slide the pizza into the oven and close the door so the oven temperature doesn't drop too much.) Bake the pizza until the crust is crisp and golden brown, 10 minutes. Using a pizza peel, lift the pizza off the screen or pan and place the crust directly on the baking stone. Using the peel or wearing thick oven mitts, remove the screen or pan from the oven. Bake the pizza until the bottom of the crust is golden brown, about 3 minutes longer. Using the peel, remove the pizza from the oven and transfer to a cutting board.

6   Scatter the lettuce over the pizza and arrange the tomato slices evenly over the lettuce. Distribute the Parmesan shavings over the top. Slice the pizza into wedges and serve immediately.

COOK'S NOTE

We experimented with seven different store-bought Caesar dressings. Some were too thin, some were too acidic, and some weren't creamy enough for the pizza. Our favorite for making this pizza is Marie's Caesar dressing, which is made with no preservatives. Look for it in the refrigerated case in the produce aisle of most supermarkets.

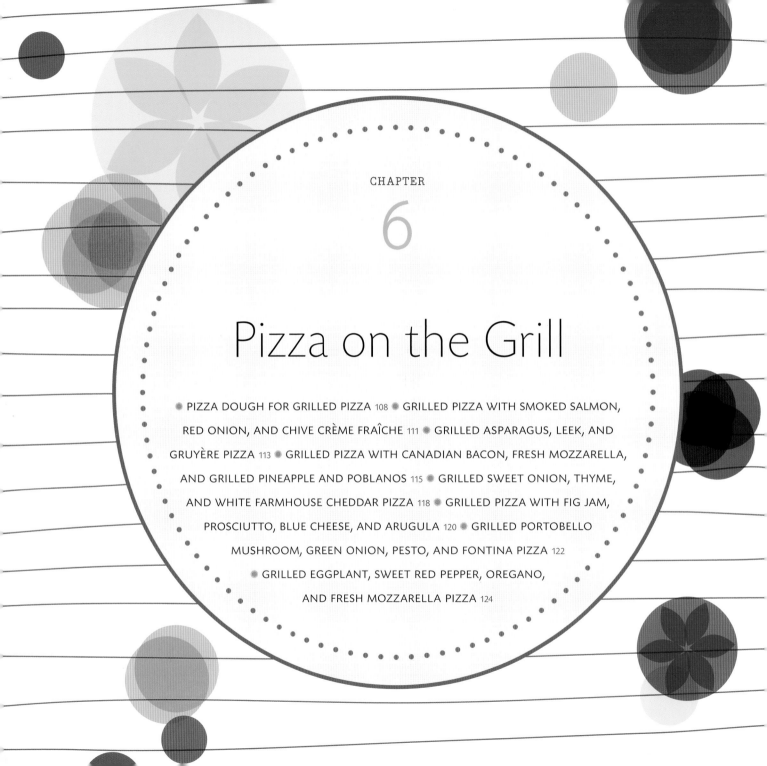

CHAPTER

6

Pizza on the Grill

Grilled pizza is exciting to make.

It takes some finesse, a little daring, definite organization of ingredients, and some critical tools. That said, it's worth practicing and mastering the techniques, because grilled pizza is uniquely delicious, with a crack and snap to the crust and a smoky flavor beyond compare.

Many think grilled pizza originated in California—with all the sunny weather, warm days, and designer pizzas on restaurant menus, pizza from the grill seems a natural. However, the restaurant generally credited with inventing grilled pizza is Al Forno in Providence, Rhode Island, owned by George Germon and Johanne Killeen. They started making grilled pizza in the early 1980s. Diane has eaten there on several occasions, and even took a class from George when he taught pizza on the grill to a group of food professionals during a conference in Providence.

The difference between grilled pizza and baking a pizza in the oven is that the dough for a grilled pizza is baked on one side before any toppings are added, whereas a pizza baked in the oven has all the toppings added before it is slid into the oven. This is why the organization of ingredients is important. Once the pizza dough is cooked on one side, the crust is flipped so the baked side with the grill marks is facing up. The toppings are added to this side, and then the pizza is slid back onto the grill to cook the underside of the crust and bake the toppings. Having the prepared ingredients ready right next to the grill is one of the keys to success.

We mentioned daring and finesse—we should also mention fun. If you have practiced sliding a pizza from a pizza peel onto a baking stone, then sliding a pizza onto a hot, well-oiled grill surface is similar. The difference is you have a hot live fire to deal with, and you want the dough to land in the right place. For your first time, try making smaller, individual pizzas by cutting the dough in half and rolling out two crusts. This way you'll be sliding a smaller piece of dough onto the grill. Another trick is to make an extra batch of dough so you have a backup supply just in case the dough folds over on itself while you're trying to slide it on the grill. Any extra dough can be frozen for later use.

There are a few special tools useful for making pizza on the grill, though we have seen many successful improvisations. Long tongs for moving the coals and sliding the pizza are very helpful, as are long oven mitts. For us, the one absolutely critical piece of equipment for pizza grilling is a pizza peel, for sliding the dough onto the grill grate and then transferring the finished pizza to a cutting board. A wooden pizza peel is charming, but for grilling pizzas, we've found a metal peel practical, as it won't burn if it touches the grill grate.

Don't wait to make pizza on the grill—it's too much fun—but you might consider trying a few practice pizzas to get the hang of it before you invite friends to a grilled pizza party.

Pizza Dough for Grilled Pizza

1 PACKAGE (2¼ TEASPOONS)
ACTIVE DRY YEAST

¾ CUP PLUS 1 TABLESPOON
LUKEWARM WATER (90° TO 100°F)

¼ CUP RYE FLOUR

2 TABLESPOONS OLIVE OIL, PLUS
MORE FOR OILING THE BOWL

¾ TEASPOON TABLE SALT OR
1¼ TEASPOONS KOSHER SALT

1¾ CUPS UNBLEACHED ALL-
PURPOSE FLOUR, PLUS MORE
FOR DUSTING

Diane has been using this dough recipe for years when making grilled pizza; it's adapted from Alice Waters's cookbook, *Chez Panisse Pasta, Pizza & Calzone.* Often, Diane will double the dough recipe so she has an extra portion to freeze for an easy weeknight meal or spur-of-the-moment entertaining. This dough is easy to work with, the texture and crispness of the crust is fabulous, and the subtle flavor that comes from the addition of rye flour makes the crust distinct and delicious. Look for rye flour in bulk at natural-foods stores. Substitute whole-wheat flour, if desired.

1   To make the dough by hand: Begin by making a sponge. In a medium bowl, dissolve the yeast in ¼ cup of the warm water. Add the rye flour and stir with a wooden spoon or rubber spatula to combine. Cover with plastic wrap and let rise in a warm place for 20 to 30 minutes. Add the remaining ½ cup plus 1 tablespoon warm water, the 2 tablespoons olive oil, salt, and 1¾ cups all-purpose flour to the sponge. Using a wooden spoon, mix the dough, incorporating as much of the flour as possible. Turn the dough out on a lightly floured work surface and knead until soft and elastic, 10 to 12 minutes. It will still be a little sticky but shouldn't stick to your hands. Add only a minimum amount of flour to the work surface to keep the dough from sticking. Generously oil a large bowl. Add the dough and turn to coat on all sides. Cover the bowl with plastic wrap and then place a clean, damp kitchen towel over the top.

To make the dough using a mixer: Fit a heavy-duty stand mixer with the dough hook attachment. In the mixer bowl, stir the yeast into ¼ cup of the warm water. Add the rye flour and mix on low speed until combined. Place a clean, damp kitchen towel over the mixer to cover the bowl and let the sponge rise for 20 minutes. Add the remaining ½ cup plus 1 tablespoon warm water, the 2 table-spoons olive oil, salt, and 1¾ cups all-purpose flour to the sponge. Mix on low speed until the flour is incorporated and the dough gathers together to form a coarse ball, about 3 minutes. Let rest for

2 minutes and then mix on medium-low speed until the dough is smooth and slightly sticky, about 3 minutes longer. Even if the dough seems too sticky, turn the dough out on a well-floured work surface and knead for a minute or two until it forms a smooth ball, adding up to 2 tablespoons of additional flour, if necessary. Generously oil a large bowl (or use the mixer bowl), add the dough, and turn to coat on all sides. Cover the bowl with plastic wrap and then place a clean, damp kitchen towel over the top.

2   Set the bowl in a warm spot (a pilot-heated oven is a good spot, or an electric oven turned to 150°F for 5 minutes and then turned off). Let the dough rise until doubled in volume, about 2 hours. Punch down the dough, cover it, and let it rise for another 40 minutes. The dough is now ready to be rolled out. (If you want to make the pizza dough ahead, after the first rising, the dough can be punched down and placed in a large lock-top plastic freezer bag. Refrigerate the dough for up to 12 hours. Bring the dough to room temperature before completing the final rise. Alternatively, freeze the dough for up to 3 months. Thaw overnight in the refrigerator and then bring the dough to room temperature before completing the final rise.)

Grilled Pizza with Smoked Salmon, Red Onion, and Chive Crème Fraîche

MAKES ONE 12-INCH PIZZA;
SERVES 4 TO 6

PIZZA DOUGH FOR GRILLED PIZZA
(PAGE 108), AT ROOM TEMPERATURE

¼ CUP SNIPPED FRESH CHIVES

½ CUP CRÈME FRAÎCHE

½ LARGE RED ONION, THINLY
SLICED

¼ CUP EXTRA-VIRGIN OLIVE OIL

1 TEASPOON KOSHER SALT

FRESHLY GROUND PEPPER

4 OUNCES SMOKED SALMON
(LOX), SLICED PAPER-THIN

2 TABLESPOONS CHOPPED
FRESH DILL

FLOUR AND MEDIUM-GRIND
YELLOW CORNMEAL FOR DUSTING

VEGETABLE OIL FOR BRUSHING

Perfect for casual summer parties, a pizza on the grill is something everyone enjoys watching. This pizza also makes a great appetizer, cut into narrow wedges and served with a cold sparkling Prosecco or French Chardonnay.

1   Have the pizza dough covered and ready to roll out. In a small bowl, combine the chives and crème fraîche. Set aside.

2   In a medium bowl, mix the red onion with the olive oil, salt, and a few grindings of pepper. Set aside.

3   Remove the salmon from the refrigerator, separate the slices, and arrange on a plate, ready for topping the pizza. Have the dill in a small bowl ready for garnishing.

4   Prepare a hot fire in a charcoal grill or preheat the center burner of a gas grill on high and the front and back or side burners to medium-low. Generously dust a pizza peel or large rimless baking sheet with flour and then cornmeal. Have all the pizza toppings set out next to the grill before rolling out the dough.

5   Flatten the dough on a lightly floured work surface, sprinkling a couple of tablespoons of cornmeal over the flour. Using a rolling pin, roll the dough into a circle 12 to 13 inches in diameter. The dough should be about ¼ inch thick. If the dough shrinks back at the edges, gently stretch it by hand, being careful to keep the dough a uniform thickness. (The dough does not need to be a perfect circle; in fact, an odd-shaped circle gives the pizza a lovely rustic look.)

continued on next page →

6   Using your hands and working quickly, lift and transfer the dough to the pizza peel or baking sheet. Give the peel or sheet a few shakes back and forth to make sure the dough isn't sticking. Brush the grill rack generously with vegetable oil. Slide the dough onto the center of the grill rack, using a quick jerking motion with your arm. If any part of the dough folds over on itself, use a pair of tongs to unfold it. Immediately cover the grill. Grill until a crust forms and light grill marks appear, 1 to 2 minutes.

7   Using the pizza peel or baking sheet, flip the pizza crust over and pull it off the grill. Cover the grill while adding the toppings. (If using a charcoal grill, shovel some of the charcoal to one side to create a cooler section. If using a gas grill, turn the center burner to medium.)

8   Spread the onion mixture evenly over the lightly charred crust. Using a spoon, drop dollops of the crème fraîche mixture over the onion. Slide the pizza back on the grill toward the hot section, but not directly over it. Cover the grill and bake the pizza until nicely browned and crisp on the bottom and at the edges, about 7 minutes. Check the pizza after about 3 minutes. If the pizza is browning too quickly, slide it over to the cooler part of the grill to finish baking. Arrange the slices of salmon over the onion mixture and garnish with the dill. Cover the grill and bake 1 minute longer. Remove any excess flour and cornmeal from the pizza peel or baking sheet and use it to transfer the pizza to a cutting board. Slice the pizza into wedges and serve immediately.

Grilled Asparagus, Leek, and Gruyère Pizza

MAKES ONE 12-INCH PIZZA;
SERVES 4 TO 6

PIZZA DOUGH FOR GRILLED PIZZA
(*PAGE 108*), AT ROOM TEMPERATURE

14 THIN SPEARS ASPARAGUS,
TOUGH ENDS REMOVED

4 LEEKS, WHITE AND LIGHT
GREEN PARTS ONLY, HALVED
LENGTHWISE

OLIVE OIL FOR BRUSHING AND
DRIZZLING

KOSHER SALT

FRESHLY GROUND PEPPER

4 OUNCES GRUYÈRE CHEESE,
THINLY SLICED

3 TABLESPOONS GRATED
PARMESAN CHEESE, PREFERABLY
PARMIGIANO-REGGIANO

With the grill fired up, it makes perfect sense to grill some of the toppings before you make a pizza. Grilling is one of our favorite ways to cook asparagus. The spears stay crisp-tender and brilliant green, with light grill marks. If you close the cover to the grill for just a moment while grilling the vegetables, the asparagus and leeks will pick up a lovely, smoky flavor. Paired with the nutty, rich flavor of Gruyère cheese, this is a heavenly combination—a little like an asparagus gratin on a crust.

1   Have the pizza dough covered and ready to roll out.

2   Prepare a hot fire in a charcoal grill or preheat the center burner of a gas grill on high and the front and back or side burners to medium-low. Lay the asparagus and leeks in a single layer on a rimmed baking sheet. Brush on all sides with olive oil and season with salt and pepper. Place the vegetables in a single layer directly over the hot fire. Grill the vegetables on one side just until grill marks appear, about 3 minutes. Turn and grill until tender but still firm, about 2 minutes longer. Remove the vegetables from the grill. Cut the leeks into long, thin strips. Set the vegetables next to the grill along with the Gruyère and Parmesan.

3   Generously dust a pizza peel or large, rimless baking sheet with flour and then cornmeal. Flatten the dough on a heavily floured work surface, sprinkling a couple of tablespoons of cornmeal over the flour. Using a rolling pin, roll the dough into a circle 12 to 13 inches in diameter. The dough should be about ¼ inch thick. If the dough shrinks back at the edges, gently stretch it by hand, being careful to keep the dough a uniform thickness. (The dough does not need to be a perfect circle; in fact, an odd-shaped circle gives the pizza a lovely rustic look.)

4   Using your hands and working quickly, lift and transfer the dough to the pizza peel or baking sheet. Give the peel or sheet a few shakes back and forth to make sure the dough isn't sticking. Brush the grill rack generously with vegetable oil. Slide the dough onto the center of the grill rack, using a quick jerking motion with your arm. If any part of the dough folds over on itself, use a pair of tongs to unfold it. Immediately cover the grill. Grill until a crust forms and light grill marks appear, 1 to 2 minutes.

continued on next page →

FLOUR AND MEDIUM-GRIND
YELLOW CORNMEAL FOR
DUSTING

VEGETABLE OIL FOR BRUSHING

5   Using the pizza peel or baking sheet, flip the pizza crust over and pull it off the grill. Cover the grill while adding the toppings. (If using a charcoal grill, shovel some of the charcoal to one side to create a cooler section. If using a gas grill, turn the center burner to medium.)

6   Drizzle a bit of olive oil evenly over the lightly charred crust. Arrange the asparagus artfully over the pizza crust and scatter the leeks over the top. Evenly distribute the Gruyère over the vegetables and sprinkle the Parmesan over the top. Slide the pizza back on the grill toward the hot section, but not directly over it. Cover the grill and bake the pizza until nicely browned and crisp on the bottom and at the edges and the cheese has melted, about 7 minutes. Check the pizza after about 3 minutes. If the pizza is browning too quickly, slide it over to the cooler part of the grill to finish baking. Remove any excess flour and cornmeal from the pizza peel or baking sheet and use it to transfer the pizza to a cutting board. Slice the pizza into wedges and serve immediately.

Grilled Pizza with Canadian Bacon, Fresh Mozzarella, and Grilled Pineapple and Poblanos

MAKES ONE 12-INCH PIZZA;
SERVES 4 TO 6

PIZZA DOUGH FOR GRILLED PIZZA
(*PAGE 108*), AT ROOM TEMPERATURE

VEGETABLE OIL FOR BRUSHING

1 SMALL, RIPE PINEAPPLE,
PEELED AND CUT CROSSWISE
INTO ¼-INCH SLICES, LEAVING
THE CORE INTACT

1 POBLANO CHILE

OLIVE OIL FOR DRIZZLING

4 OUNCES CANADIAN BACON,
THINLY SLICED

5 OUNCES FRESH WHOLE-MILK
MOZZARELLA, THINLY SLICED AND
BLOTTED WITH PAPER TOWELS TO
REMOVE EXCESS MOISTURE

FLEUR DE SEL

FRESHLY GROUND PEPPER

FLOUR AND MEDIUM-GRIND
YELLOW CORNMEAL FOR DUSTING

Taking our cue from those who love pineapple and Canadian bacon on pizza, we developed a grilled pizza with those toppings. However, we upped the intensity of flavors and not only added poblano chiles, but also grilled both the chile and the pineapple before topping the pizza. Lusty, crisp, and smoky with meltingly delicious fresh mozzarella—this is a party-worthy pizza.

1   Have the pizza dough covered and ready to roll out.

2   Prepare a hot fire in a charcoal grill or preheat the center burner of a gas grill on high and the front and back or side burners to medium-low. Brush the grill grate with vegetable oil. Arrange the pineapple slices in a single layer directly over the hot fire. Place the chile on the grill grate directly over the hot fire. Cover the grill and cook until grill marks appear on the pineapple and chile, about 3 minutes. Turn the chile and continue to char the skin. Turn the pineapple and grill until grill marks appear on the other side, 2 to 3 minutes longer. Remove the pineapple slices and set on a plate next to the grill. Turn the chile again and continue grilling until the skin is blistered and charred on all sides. Remove from the grill. Dampen a paper towel and wrap the chile in the towel until cool enough to handle, about 5 minutes. Use the paper towel to rub off

the skin. Cut the chile in half, discard the core, seeds, and ribs, and cut into long strips. Set the grilled pineapple and chile next to the grill along with the olive oil, Canadian bacon, mozzarella, salt, and pepper.

3   Generously dust a pizza peel or large rimless baking sheet with flour and then cornmeal. Flatten the dough on a heavily floured work surface, sprinkling a couple of tablespoons of cornmeal over the flour. Using a rolling pin, roll the dough into a circle 12 to 13 inches in diameter. The dough should be about ¼ inch thick. If the dough shrinks back at the edges, gently stretch it by hand, being careful to keep the dough a uniform thickness. (The dough does not need to be a perfect circle; in fact, an odd-shaped circle gives the pizza a lovely rustic look.)

continued on next page →

4   Using your hands and working quickly, lift and transfer the dough to the pizza peel or baking sheet. Give the peel or sheet a few shakes back and forth to make sure the dough isn't sticking. Brush the grill rack generously with oil. Slide the dough onto the center of the grill rack, using a quick jerking motion with your arm. If any part of the dough folds over on itself, use a pair of tongs to unfold it. Immediately cover the grill. Grill until a crust forms and light grill marks appear, 1 to 2 minutes.

5   Using the pizza peel or baking sheet, flip the pizza crust over and pull it off the grill. Cover the grill while adding the toppings. (If using a charcoal grill, shovel some of the charcoal to one side to create a cooler section. If using a gas grill, turn the center burner to medium.)

6   Drizzle a bit of olive oil evenly over the lightly charred crust. Arrange the pineapple slices evenly over the pizza crust and top with the bacon. Evenly distribute the mozzarella cheese over the top. Scatter the strips of grilled poblano over the top and season with a little fleur de sel and a few grindings of pepper. Slide the pizza back on the grill toward the hot section, but not directly over it. Cover the grill and bake the pizza until nicely browned and crisp on the bottom and at the edges and the cheese has melted, about 7 minutes. Check the pizza after about 3 minutes. If the pizza is browning too quickly, slide it over to the cooler part of the grill to finish baking. Remove any excess flour and cornmeal from the pizza peel or baking sheet and use it to transfer the pizza to a cutting board. Slice the pizza into wedges and serve immediately.

Grilled Sweet Onion, Thyme, and White Farmhouse Cheddar Pizza

MAKES ONE 12-INCH PIZZA;
SERVES 4 TO 6

PIZZA DOUGH FOR GRILLED PIZZA
(*PAGE 108*), AT ROOM TEMPERATURE

1 LARGE WALLA WALLA OR
VIDALIA ONION, CUT CROSSWISE
INTO ¼-INCH SLICES

OLIVE OIL FOR BRUSHING AND
DRIZZLING

1 TABLESPOON FRESH THYME
LEAVES

FRESHLY GROUND PEPPER

6 OUNCES WHITE FARMHOUSE
CHEDDAR CHEESE, THINLY SLICED

FLOUR AND MEDIUM-GRIND
YELLOW CORNMEAL FOR
DUSTING

VEGETABLE OIL FOR BRUSHING

Living in the Pacific Northwest, Diane grills Walla Walla sweet onions from the moment they arrive in the market. Of course, they're great served as hunky slices on top of a grilled burger or cut into wedges and skewered with a mixed grill of vegetables, but nothing beats grilled sweet onions scattered over the top of a pizza, especially when a white farmhouse Cheddar is melted over top. Fresh thyme is critical here; don't substitute dried.

1   Have the pizza dough covered and ready to roll out.

2   Prepare a hot fire in a charcoal grill or preheat the center burner of a gas grill on high and the front and back or side burners to medium-low. Lay the onion slices in a single layer on a rimmed baking sheet. Brush on both sides with olive oil. Place the onion in a single layer directly over the hot fire. Grill the onion on one side just until grill marks appear, 2 to 3 minutes. Turn and grill until tender but still firm, about 2 minutes longer. Remove the onion from the grill and set on a plate next to the grill along with the thyme, pepper, and Cheddar cheese.

3   Generously dust a pizza peel or large rimless baking sheet with flour and then cornmeal. Flatten the dough on a heavily floured work surface, sprinkling a couple of tablespoons of cornmeal over the flour. Using a rolling pin, roll the dough into a circle 12 to 13 inches in diameter. The dough should be about ¼ inch thick. If the dough shrinks back at the edges, gently stretch it by hand, being careful to keep the dough a uniform thickness. (The dough does not need to be a perfect circle; in fact, an odd-shaped circle gives the pizza a lovely rustic look.)

4   Using your hands and working quickly, lift and transfer the dough to the pizza peel or baking sheet. Give the peel or sheet a few shakes back and forth to make sure the dough isn't sticking. Brush the grill rack generously with vegetable oil. Slide the dough onto the center of the grill rack, using a quick jerking motion with your arm. If any part of the dough folds over on itself, use a pair of tongs to unfold it. Immediately cover the grill. Grill until a crust forms and light grill marks appear, 1 to 2 minutes.

5   Using the pizza peel or baking sheet, flip the pizza crust over and pull it off the grill. Cover the grill while adding the toppings. (If using a charcoal grill, shovel some of the charcoal to one side to create a cooler section. If using a gas grill, turn the center burner to medium.)

6   Drizzle a bit of olive oil evenly over the lightly charred crust. Separate the onion into rings and arrange evenly over the pizza crust. Scatter the thyme over the top and season with a few grindings of pepper. Evenly distribute the cheese over the onion. Slide the pizza back on the grill toward the hot section, but not directly over it. Cover the grill and bake the pizza until nicely browned and crisp on the bottom and at the edges and the cheese has melted, about 7 minutes. Check the pizza after about 3 minutes. If the pizza is browning too quickly, slide it over to the cooler part of the grill to finish baking. Remove any excess flour and cornmeal from the pizza peel or baking sheet and use it to transfer the pizza to a cutting board. Slice the pizza into wedges and serve immediately.

Grilled Pizza with Fig Jam, Prosciutto, Blue Cheese, and Arugula

MAKES ONE 12-INCH PIZZA;
SERVES 4 TO 6

PIZZA DOUGH FOR GRILLED PIZZA
(PAGE 108), AT ROOM TEMPERATURE

⅓ CUP FIG JAM

3 OUNCES THINLY SLICED
PROSCIUTTO DI PARMA, CUT
CROSSWISE INTO THIN STRIPS

4 OUNCES BLUE CHEESE,
CRUMBLED

1 BUNCH (ABOUT 2 OUNCES)
ARUGULA, TOUGH STEMS
REMOVED

FLOUR AND MEDIUM-GRIND
YELLOW CORNMEAL FOR DUSTING

VEGETABLE OIL FOR BRUSHING

Inspired by a main-course salad that combined grilled figs with slivers of prosciutto and blue cheese on a bed of arugula, Diane came up with this great combination for a grilled pizza. She substituted fig jam for the grilled figs so there would be a little "glue" on the crust to hold the toppings, and then scattered the prosciutto and blue cheese over top.

1   Have the pizza dough covered and ready to roll out.

2   Prepare a hot fire in a charcoal grill or preheat the center burner of a gas grill on high and the front and back or side burners to medium-low. Place the fig jam, prosciutto, blue cheese, and arugula next to the grill, ready to top the pizza.

3   Generously dust a pizza peel or large rimless baking sheet with flour and then cornmeal. Flatten the dough on a heavily floured work surface, sprinkling a couple of tablespoons of cornmeal over the flour. Using a rolling pin, roll the dough into a circle 12 to 13 inches in diameter. The dough should be about ¼ inch thick. If the dough shrinks back at the edges, gently stretch it by hand, being careful to keep the dough a uniform thickness. (The dough does not need to be a perfect circle; in fact, an odd-shaped circle gives the pizza a lovely rustic look.)

4   Using your hands and working quickly, lift and transfer the dough to the pizza peel or baking sheet. Give the peel or sheet a few shakes back and forth to make sure the dough isn't sticking. Brush the grill rack generously with oil. Slide the dough onto the center of the grill rack, using a quick jerking motion with your arm. If any part of the dough

folds over on itself, use a pair of tongs to unfold it. Immediately cover the grill. Grill until a crust forms and light grill marks appear, 1 to 2 minutes.

5   Using the pizza peel or baking sheet, flip the pizza crust over and pull it off the grill. Cover the grill while adding the toppings. (If using a charcoal grill, shovel some of the charcoal to one side to create a cooler section. If using a gas grill, turn the center burner to medium.)

6   Spread the fig jam evenly over the lightly charred crust, leaving a 1-inch border. Scatter the prosciutto over the top. Evenly distribute the blue cheese over the prosciutto. Slide the pizza back on the grill toward the hot section but not directly over it. Cover the grill and bake the pizza until nicely browned and crisp on the bottom and at the edges and the cheese has melted, about 7 minutes. Check the pizza after about 3 minutes. If the pizza is browning too quickly, slide it over to the cooler part of the grill to finish baking. Remove any excess flour and cornmeal from the pizza peel or baking sheet and use it to transfer the pizza to a cutting board. Distribute the arugula evenly over the pizza. Slice the pizza into wedges and serve immediately.

Grilled Portobello Mushroom, Green Onion, Pesto, and Fontina Pizza

MAKES ONE 12-INCH PIZZA;
SERVES 4 TO 6

PIZZA DOUGH FOR GRILLED PIZZA
(*PAGE 108*), AT ROOM TEMPERATURE

¼ CUP PESTO, HOMEMADE
(*PAGE 53*) OR STORE-BOUGHT

2 TABLESPOONS EXTRA-VIRGIN
OLIVE OIL, PLUS MORE FOR
BRUSHING

3 LARGE PORTOBELLO MUSH-
ROOMS, STEMS AND BLACK GILLS
REMOVED

1 BUNCH (*ABOUT 8*) GREEN
ONIONS, ENDS TRIMMED

4 OUNCES ITALIAN FONTINA
CHEESE, THINLY SLICED

FRESHLY GROUND PEPPER

FLOUR AND MEDIUM-GRIND
YELLOW CORNMEAL FOR DUSTING

VEGETABLE OIL FOR BRUSHING

Picture a terrific grilled portobello mushroom burger topped with melted fontina cheese, layered with grilled green onions, and the bun slathered with pesto. That mouthwatering combo is reinvented as the toppings for this pizza—the portobellos are grilled and then sliced, the pesto is spread over the smoky, crackly-crisp pizza crust, and the toppings are scattered over the top under meltingly delicious Italian fontina cheese.

1   Have the pizza dough covered and ready to roll out. In a bowl, combine the pesto and 2 tablespoons olive oil. Set aside.

2   Prepare a hot fire in a charcoal grill or preheat the center burner of a gas grill on high and the front and back or side burners to medium-low. Arrange the mushrooms and green onions in a single layer on a rimmed baking sheet. Brush on both sides with olive oil. Place the vegetables in a single layer directly over the hot fire. Grill on one side just until grill marks appear, about 2 minutes for the green onions, 3 to 4 minutes for the mush-rooms. Turn and grill until tender but still firm, 2 to 3 minutes longer. Remove the onions from the grill and set them on a plate next to the grill. Transfer the mushrooms to a cutting board and cut into ½-inch strips. Set next to the grill along with the fontina and pepper.

3   Generously dust a pizza peel or large rimless baking sheet with flour and then cornmeal. Flatten the dough on a heavily floured work surface, sprinkling a couple of tablespoons of cornmeal over the flour. Using a rolling pin, roll the dough into a circle 12 to 13 inches in diameter. The dough should be about ¼ inch thick. If the dough shrinks back at the edges, gently stretch it by hand, being careful to keep the dough a uniform thickness. (The dough does not need to be a perfect circle; in fact, an odd-shaped circle gives the pizza a lovely rustic look.)

4   Using your hands and working quickly, lift and transfer the dough to the pizza peel or baking sheet. Give the peel or sheet a few shakes back and forth to make sure the dough isn't sticking. Brush the grill rack generously with vegetable oil. Slide the dough onto the center of the grill rack, using a quick jerking motion with your arm. If any part of the dough folds over on itself, use a pair of tongs to unfold it. Immediately cover the grill. Grill until a crust forms and light grill marks appear, 1 to 2 minutes.

5   Using the pizza peel, flip the pizza crust over and pull it off the grill. Cover the grill while adding the toppings. (If using a charcoal grill, shovel some of the charcoal to one side to create a cooler section. If using a gas grill, turn the center burner to medium.)

6   Spread the pesto evenly over the lightly charred crust, leaving a 1-inch border. Arrange the mushrooms evenly over the pesto-coated crust. Arrange the fontina slices evenly over the mushrooms. Season with a few grindings of pepper. Slide the pizza back on the grill toward the hot section, but not directly over it. Cover the grill and bake the pizza until nicely browned and crisp on the bottom and at the edges and the cheese has melted, about 7 minutes. Check the pizza after about 3 minutes. If the pizza is browning too quickly, slide it over to the cooler part of the grill to finish baking. Remove any excess flour and cornmeal from the pizza peel or baking sheet and use it to transfer the pizza to a cutting board. Artfully scatter the green onions over top. Slice the pizza into wedges and serve immediately.

Grilled Eggplant, Sweet Red Pepper, Oregano, and Fresh Mozzarella Pizza

MAKES ONE 12-INCH PIZZA;
SERVES 4 TO 6

Here is the heart of late summer on a pizza: market-fresh eggplant and red peppers sliced, grilled, and intertwined with warm melted mozzarella; fresh herbs; dots of capers; and drizzles of olive oil. This is grilled pizza as it was meant to be, every bite a sensual taste pleasure.

PIZZA DOUGH FOR GRILLED PIZZA
(*PAGE 108*), AT ROOM TEMPERATURE

1 MEDIUM EGGPLANT, CUT
CROSSWISE INTO ¼-INCH SLICES

2 TO 3 TABLESPOONS ROASTED
GARLIC–FLAVORED EXTRA-VIRGIN
OLIVE OIL, PLUS MORE FOR
DRIZZLING

1 LARGE RED BELL PEPPER

2 TABLESPOONS CAPERS, DRAINED

3 TABLESPOONS CHOPPED FRESH
OREGANO

2 TABLESPOONS CHOPPED FRESH
FLAT-LEAF PARSLEY

1   Have the pizza dough covered and ready to roll out.

2   Prepare a hot fire in a charcoal grill or preheat the center burner of a gas grill on high and the front and back or side burners to medium-low. Lay the eggplant slices in a single layer on a rimmed baking sheet. Brush generously on both sides with olive oil. Arrange the eggplant slices in a single layer directly over the hot fire. Place the bell pepper on the grill grate directly over the fire. Cover the grill and cook until grill marks appear, about 3 minutes. Turn the pepper and continue to char the skin. Turn the eggplant and grill until grill marks appear on the other side, 2 to 3 minutes longer. Remove the eggplant slices and set on a plate next to the grill. Turn the pepper again and continue grilling until the skin is blistered and charred on all sides. Remove from the grill. Dampen a paper towel and wrap the pepper in the towel until cool enough to handle, about 5 minutes. Use the paper towel to rub off the skin.

Cut the pepper in half, discard the core, seeds, and ribs, and cut into long strips. Set the grilled vegetables next to the grill along with the capers, oregano, parsley, mozzarella, salt, and pepper.

3   Generously dust a pizza peel or large rimless baking sheet with flour and then cornmeal. Flatten the dough on a heavily floured work surface, sprinkling a couple of tablespoons of cornmeal over the flour. Using a rolling pin, roll the dough into a circle 12 to 13 inches in diameter. The dough should be about ¼ inch thick. If the dough shrinks back at the edges, gently stretch it by hand, being careful to keep the dough a uniform thickness. (The dough does not need to be a perfect circle; in fact, an odd-shaped circle gives the pizza a lovely rustic look.)

7 OUNCES FRESH WHOLE-MILK
MOZZARELLA, THINLY SLICED AND
BLOTTED WITH PAPER TOWELS TO
REMOVE EXCESS MOISTURE

FLEUR DE SEL

FRESHLY GROUND PEPPER

FLOUR AND MEDIUM-GRIND
YELLOW CORNMEAL FOR DUSTING

VEGETABLE OIL FOR BRUSHING

4   Using your hands and working quickly, lift and transfer the dough to the pizza peel or baking sheet. Give the peel or sheet a few shakes back and forth to make sure the dough isn't sticking. Brush the grill rack generously with vegetable oil. Slide the dough onto the center of the grill rack, using a quick jerking motion with your arm. If any part of the dough folds over on itself, use a pair of tongs to unfold it. Immediately cover the grill. Grill until a crust forms and light grill marks appear, 1 to 2 minutes.

5   Using the pizza peel or baking sheet, flip the pizza crust over and pull it off the grill. Cover the grill while adding the toppings. (If using a charcoal grill, shovel some of the charcoal to one side to create a cooler section. If using a gas grill, turn the center burner to medium.)

6   Drizzle a little of the olive oil evenly over the lightly charred crust. Arrange the eggplant slices evenly over the pizza crust. Evenly distribute the bell pepper strips over the eggplant. Scatter the capers, oregano, and parsley over top. Arrange the mozzarella slices evenly over the vegetables. Season with a little salt and a few grindings of pepper. Slide the pizza back on the grill toward the hot section, but not directly over it. Cover the grill and bake the pizza until nicely browned and crisp on the bottom and at the edges and the cheese has melted, about 7 minutes. Check the pizza after about 3 minutes. If the pizza is browning too quickly, slide it over to the cooler part of the grill to finish baking. Remove any excess flour and cornmeal from the pizza peel or baking sheet and use it to transfer the pizza to a cutting board. Slice the pizza into wedges and serve immediately.

CHAPTER

7

Quick and Kid-Friendly Pizza

Is it those crazy and rushed

weeknight meals, or the unexpected guests, or the spur-of-the moment kids' sleepovers that have us reaching for a little kitchen magic? Just a few tricks up a sleeve for putting a meal on the table and getting hungry tummies satisfied would really help. Pulling a frozen pizza from the freezer might do, but if you have become as hooked on pizza as we are, then turn to this chapter for quick dinner solutions when what you want is a pizza that tastes homemade but doesn't require a lot of time.

We have filled this chapter with easy, lip-smackingly delicious homemade pizzas using high-quality premade crusts as a timesaver. These premade crusts, predominantly made by Boboli, aren't frozen or refrigerated, but are sold fresh like bread. They're ready to be topped, placed on a pizza pan, popped in the oven, and baked. Almost every pizza in this chapter can be assembled in 20 minutes—the time it takes the oven to preheat.

If you maintain a well-stocked pantry with premade crusts, tasty toppings, and condiments, and you have cheese in the refrigerator ready to grate, you are ready for last-minute meals. Frozen pizza dough requires some advanced planning in order for the dough to thaw and rise, and refrigerated dough needs time to warm to room temperature before it can be rolled and stretched. Premade crusts jump-start the pizza-making process.

In addition, we think the quickest dinners are the ones where the entrée is an entire meal in itself. Like a casserole or stew, pizza can be a meal-in-one supper with the right combination of toppings. Add vegetables, some meat, cheese (of course), and with a good crust you've covered all the food groups. All the recipes in this chapter fill that bill. Our Very Veggie Pizza with Olives and Artichoke Hearts on page 135 is a perfect vegetarian supper. With any of these pizzas, add a salad or some fruit for an easy side dish if you like.

Pizza is finger food, making it naturally kid-friendly. Pizzas can be as simple or as complex as taste buds please. For very young children, cheese may be the only topping they like. In that case, half a pizza can be made with cheese and the other half with pepperoni and mushrooms to please adult tastes. Teenagers (and teenagers at heart) love pizza any time of day, so we have included a Weekend Breakfast Pizza with Link Sausage and Sunny-Side-Up Eggs on page 132 to satisfy the morning-pizza cravings. For children who like breakfast at dinnertime, especially on Sunday night, try our South of the Border Breakfast-for-Dinner Pizza on page 131.

In fact, almost every pizza in this book is adaptable to the quick-dinner approach to homemade pizza. Look beyond this chapter for other ideas.

Cheese and Pepperoni Pizza Supreme

A pizza cookbook wouldn't be complete without a cheese and pepperoni pizza. We've spiced it up a bit with the addition of peperoncini, medium-hot pickled green peppers. That, of course, is an optional topping, or add it to only half the pizza if you are serving children, too.

ONE 12-INCH BOBOLI PIZZA CRUST

3 OUNCES PEPPERONI, THINLY SLICED

½ POUND BUTTON MUSHROOMS, WIPED OR BRUSHED CLEAN, THINLY SLICED

2 PLUM TOMATOES, CORED AND THINLY SLICED

12 PEPERONCINI, THICKLY SLICED

2 CUPS (8 OUNCES) COARSELY SHREDDED WHOLE-MILK OR PART-SKIM, LOW-MOISTURE MOZZARELLA CHEESE

1 Position an oven rack in the center of the oven and place a baking stone, if using one, on the rack. Preheat the oven to 500°F.

2 Remove the Boboli from the plastic bag and set aside the packet of tomato sauce. Place the pizza crust on a pizza screen, pizza pan, or rimless baking sheet, or on a pizza peel ready to slide directly onto the baking stone.

3 To top the pizza: Spread the pizza sauce over the crust, leaving a 1-inch border. Arrange the pepperoni in a single layer over the sauce. Scatter the mushrooms over the top. Arrange the tomatoes in a single layer over the mushrooms. Scatter the peperoncini over the top. Distribute the cheese evenly over the vegetables, leaving a 1-inch border.

4 Place the pizza in the oven on the rack or stone. (Work quickly to slide the pizza into the oven and close the door so the oven temperature doesn't drop too much.) Bake the pizza until the crust is crisp and a deep golden brown and the cheese is golden, 10 to 12 minutes. Slice the pizza into wedges and serve immediately.

Canadian Bacon, Mozzarella, Pineapple, and Peperoncini Pizza

MAKES ONE 12-INCH PIZZA;
SERVES 4 TO 6

ONE 12-INCH BOBOLI PIZZA CRUST

2 CUPS (*8 OUNCES*) COARSELY
SHREDDED WHOLE-MILK OR
PART-SKIM, LOW-MOISTURE
MOZZARELLA CHEESE

3 GREEN ONIONS, THINLY SLICED

¼ POUND CANADIAN BACON,
THINLY SLICED

1 CAN (*8 OUNCES*) PINEAPPLE
CHUNKS, WELL DRAINED

12 PEPERONCINI, LEFT WHOLE OR
THICKLY SLICED

Here's a spiced-up version of the classic pizza with pineapple and Canadian bacon. Sliced green onions add a flourish of color and a pep of flavor while the peperoncini scattered on top fuel the taste buds and balance the sweetness of the pineapple. It's a winning tropical pizza combo.

1   Position an oven rack in the center of the oven and place a baking stone, if using one, on the rack. Preheat the oven to 500°F.

2   Remove the Boboli from the plastic bag and save the packet of tomato sauce for another use. Place the pizza crust on a pizza screen, pizza pan, or rimless baking sheet, or on a pizza peel ready to slide directly onto the baking stone.

3   To top the pizza: Distribute the cheese evenly over the pizza crust, leaving a 1-inch border. Scatter the green onions over the cheese. Distribute the bacon in a single layer over the top. Arrange the pineapple chunks over the bacon.

4   Place the pizza in the oven on the rack or stone. (Work quickly to slide the pizza into the oven and close the door so the oven temperature doesn't drop too much.) Bake the pizza until the crust is crisp and a deep golden brown and the cheese is golden, about 10 minutes. Scatter the peperoncini over the pizza. Slice the pizza into wedges and serve immediately.

South of the Border Breakfast-for-Dinner Pizza

MAKES ONE 12-INCH PIZZA;
SERVES 4

Playing on the huevos rancheros theme, we created a pizza with chiles, onions, pepper Jack cheese, and chorizo, all topped with over-easy eggs, drizzles of hot sauce, and a mound of salsa. If that doesn't get a crowd of big eaters to the table in a hurry we don't know what will.

ONE 12-INCH BOBOLI PIZZA CRUST

¼ CUP CANNED CHOPPED GREEN CHILES (*DICED JALAPEÑOS*), DRAINED

⅓ CUP CHOPPED WHITE ONION

2 CUPS (*8 OUNCES*) COARSELY SHREDDED PEPPER JACK CHEESE

6 OUNCES UNCOOKED CHORIZO, CUT INTO ½-INCH CHUNKS

2 TABLESPOONS UNSALTED BUTTER

4 LARGE EGGS

KOSHER SALT

FRESHLY GROUND PEPPER

TABASCO, CHOLULA, OR OTHER HOT SAUCE FOR SERVING

SALSA FOR SERVING (*OPTIONAL*)

1   Position an oven rack in the center of the oven and place a baking stone, if using one, on the rack. Preheat the oven to 500°F.

2   Remove the Boboli from the plastic bag and set aside the packet of tomato sauce. Place the pizza crust on a pizza screen, pizza pan, or rimless baking sheet, or on a pizza peel ready to slide directly onto the baking stone.

3   To top the pizza: Spread the pizza sauce over the crust, leaving a 1-inch border. Distribute the chiles and onion evenly over the sauce. Distribute the cheese evenly over the top. Arrange the chunks of chorizo in a single layer over the cheese, pressing them lightly into the cheese.

4   Place the pizza in the oven on the rack or stone. (Work quickly to slide the pizza into the oven and close the door so the oven temperature doesn't drop too much.) Bake the pizza until the crust is crisp and a deep golden brown and the cheese is golden, about 10 minutes.

5   When the pizza is about 4 minutes from being done, melt the butter in a medium skillet, preferably nonstick, over medium heat. Crack the eggs into the pan and sprinkle lightly with salt and a few grindings of pepper. Cook until the whites are set and the yolks are heated through but still runny. (Turn the eggs over if you want them over-easy.) Cut the pizza into fourths and transfer to warm plates. Using a spatula, slide an egg, sunny-side up (or over-easy), onto the top of each slice of pizza. Serve immediately, passing the hot sauce to drizzle over the top and salsa, if desired.

Weekend Breakfast Pizza with Link Sausage and Sunny-Side-Up Eggs

MAKES ONE 12-INCH PIZZA;
SERVES 4

Who says pizza is only for lunch and dinner? Here's a hearty breakfast pizza to start a weekend day. This pizza got rave reviews when tested on Diane's son and his group of friends. For those who love to start a lazy Sunday with toast, sausage, and eggs, here is a terrific alternative.

ONE 12-INCH BOBOLI PIZZA CRUST

2 CUPS (8 OUNCES) COARSELY
SHREDDED WHOLE-MILK OR
PART-SKIM, LOW-MOISTURE
MOZZARELLA CHEESE

7 PORK LINK BREAKFAST
SAUSAGES (ABOUT 6 OUNCES),
CUT INTO ¾-INCH LENGTHS

2 TABLESPOONS UNSALTED
BUTTER

4 LARGE EGGS

KOSHER SALT

FRESHLY GROUND PEPPER

2 GREEN ONIONS, THINLY SLICED
(OPTIONAL)

TABASCO, CHOLULA, OR OTHER
HOT SAUCE FOR SERVING

1   Position an oven rack in the center of the oven and place a baking stone, if using one, on the rack. Preheat the oven to 500°F.

2   Remove the Boboli from the plastic bag and set aside the packet of tomato sauce. Place the pizza crust on a pizza screen, pizza pan, or rimless baking sheet, or on a pizza peel ready to slide directly onto the baking stone.

3   To top the pizza: Spread the pizza sauce over the crust, leaving a 1-inch border. Distribute the cheese evenly over the sauce. Arrange the chunks of sausage in a single layer over the cheese, pressing them lightly into the cheese.

4   Place the pizza in the oven on the rack or stone. (Work quickly to slide the pizza into the oven and close the door so the oven temperature doesn't drop too much.) Bake the pizza until the crust is crisp and a deep golden brown and the cheese is golden, about 10 minutes.

5   When the pizza is about 4 minutes from being done, melt the butter in a medium skillet, preferably nonstick, over medium heat. Crack the eggs into the pan and sprinkle lightly with salt and a few grindings of pepper. Cook until the whites are set and the yolks are heated through but still runny. (Turn the eggs over if you want them over-easy.) Cut the pizza into fourths and transfer to warm plates. Using a spatula, slide an egg, sunny-side up (or over-easy), onto the top of each slice of pizza. Scatter the green onions over the eggs, if desired. Serve immediately, passing the hot sauce to drizzle over the top.

Crossing-Cultures Chinese Hoisin Pizza

MAKES ONE 12-INCH PIZZA;
SERVES 4 TO 6

Layers of sweet, smoky, pungent flavors are blanketed with cheese and baked to crusty pizza perfection. The top of the pizza is bejeweled with a shower of cilantro. This isn't fusion confusion—this is an Asian pizza delight.

1¾ CUPS SHREDDED SAUTÉED OR ROAST CHICKEN

3 TABLESPOONS, PLUS ¼ CUP HOISIN SAUCE

2 TEASPOONS MINCED GARLIC

1 TABLESPOON MINCED FRESH GINGER

1 TEASPOON *SAMBAL OELEK* (SEE COOK'S NOTE)

6 GREEN ONIONS, INCLUDING GREEN TOPS, CUT ON THE DIAGONAL INTO THIN SLICES

ONE 12-INCH BOBOLI PIZZA CRUST

1 CUP THINLY SLICED WHITE ONION

1½ CUPS (6 OUNCES) COARSELY SHREDDED WHOLE-MILK OR PART-SKIM, LOW-MOISTURE MOZZARELLA CHEESE

½ CUP LIGHTLY PACKED CILANTRO LEAVES

1   Position an oven rack in the center of the oven and place a baking stone, if using one, on the rack. Preheat the oven to 500°F.

2   While the oven is heating, toss the shredded chicken with the 3 tablespoons hoisin, the garlic, ginger, *sambal oelek,* and 3 of the green onions.

3   Remove the Boboli from the plastic bag and save the packet of tomato sauce for another use. Place the pizza crust on a pizza screen, pizza pan, or rimless baking sheet, or on a pizza peel ready to slide directly onto the baking stone.

4   To top the pizza: Spread the ¼ cup hoisin sauce evenly over the pizza crust, leaving a 1-inch border. Distribute the white onion over the sauce. Arrange the chicken mixture in a single layer over the onion. Distribute the cheese evenly over the top.

5   Place the pizza in the oven on the rack or stone. (Work quickly to slide the pizza into the oven and close the door so the oven temperature doesn't drop too much.) Bake the pizza until the crust is crisp and a deep golden brown and the cheese is golden, about 10 minutes. Scatter the remaining green onions and the cilantro over the pizza. Slice the pizza into wedges and serve immediately.

COOK'S NOTE

Sambal oelek is an Indonesian hot chile pepper paste made from chiles, salt, vinegar, and sometimes garlic and tamarind as well. It is a fiery paste with bright flavors—a little goes a long way. Other Asian chile pastes with garlic can be substituted, but this one is a favorite of ours. Keep refrigerated once opened; it will keep indefinitely.

Very Veggie Pizza with Olives and Artichoke Hearts

MAKES ONE 12-INCH PIZZA;
SERVES 4 TO 6

We call this pizza "very veggie" for good reason: It's packed with colorful veggies given a flavor boost by tossing them with some extra-virgin olive oil and herbs. As if the medley of zucchini, onion, and bell pepper weren't enough of a vitamin boost, we also added tomatoes, artichokes, and olives. Pack all this under the cheese and bake it for a meltingly delicious vegetarian pizza.

1 SMALL ZUCCHINI, THINLY SLICED

½ SMALL WHITE ONION, CUT INTO THIN WEDGES

1 SMALL YELLOW BELL PEPPER, SEEDED, DERIBBED, AND CUT INTO LONG THIN STRIPS

2 TABLESPOONS EXTRA-VIRGIN OLIVE OIL

1 TEASPOON DRIED OREGANO

¼ TEASPOON KOSHER SALT

½ TEASPOON RED PEPPER FLAKES

ONE 12-INCH BOBOLI PIZZA CRUST

1   Position an oven rack in the center of the oven and place a baking stone, if using one, on the rack. Preheat the oven to 500°F.

2   While the oven is heating, place the zucchini, onion, and bell pepper in a medium bowl. Toss the vegetables with the olive oil, oregano, salt, and red pepper flakes. Set aside.

3   Remove the Boboli from the plastic bag and set aside the packet of tomato sauce. Place the pizza crust on a pizza screen, pizza pan, or rimless baking sheet, or on a pizza peel ready to slide directly onto the baking stone.

continued on next page ➜

1 JAR *(6 OUNCES)* MARINATED ARTICHOKE HEARTS, WELL DRAINED AND HALVED

....

2 PLUM TOMATOES, CORED AND THINLY SLICED

....

⅓ CUP HALVED AND PITTED CANNED RIPE BLACK OLIVES

....

2 CUPS *(8 OUNCES)* COARSELY SHREDDED WHOLE-MILK OR PART-SKIM, LOW-MOISTURE MOZZARELLA CHEESE

....

4 To top the pizza: Spread the pizza sauce over the crust, leaving a 1-inch border. Arrange the vegetables evenly over the sauce. Scatter the artichokes over the top. Arrange the tomatoes in a single layer over the vegetables. Scatter the olives over the top. Distribute the cheese evenly over the vegetables.

5 Place the pizza in the oven on the rack or stone. (Work quickly to slide the pizza into the oven and close the door so the oven temperature doesn't drop too much.) Bake the pizza until the crust is crisp and a deep golden brown and the cheese is golden, 10 to 12 minutes. Slice the pizza into wedges and serve immediately.

Garlic-Marinated Shrimp, Sweet Onion, and Roasted Red Pepper Pesto Pizza

MAKES ONE 12-INCH PIZZA;
SERVES 4 TO 6

This is a pizza worthy of a party. Doused with a lemon-garlic–red pepper infusion, glistening pink shrimp swim atop layers of sweet onions and bell peppers, and a hefty mound of rich melted cheese. A pizza lover's pleasure with crunch, fresh and vibrant flavors, and heady herbal aromas.

1 POUND LARGE SHRIMP, PEELED, DEVEINED, AND HALVED LENGTHWISE

2 TABLESPOONS EXTRA-VIRGIN OLIVE OIL

1 TABLESPOON FRESH LEMON JUICE

1 TABLESPOON MINCED GARLIC

½ TO ¾ TEASPOON RED PEPPER FLAKES

ONE 12-INCH BOBOLI PIZZA CRUST

⅔ CUP ROASTED RED PEPPER PESTO, HOMEMADE (PAGE 139) OR STORE-BOUGHT

½ MEDIUM WALLA WALLA OR VIDALIA ONION, CUT INTO THIN WEDGES

1 SMALL RED BELL PEPPER, SEEDED, DERIBBED, AND CUT INTO LONG THIN STRIPS

2 CUPS (8 OUNCES) COARSELY SHREDDED WHOLE-MILK OR PART-SKIM, LOW-MOISTURE MOZZARELLA CHEESE

10 FRESH BASIL LEAVES, TORN INTO LARGE PIECES

1 Position an oven rack in the center of the oven and place a baking stone, if using one, on the rack. Preheat the oven to 500°F.

2 While the oven is heating, in a bowl, toss the shrimp with the olive oil, lemon juice, garlic, and red pepper flakes.

3 Remove the Boboli from the plastic bag and save the packet of tomato sauce for another use. Place the pizza crust on a pizza screen, pizza pan, or rimless baking sheet, or on a pizza peel ready to slide directly onto the baking stone.

4 To top the pizza: Spread the pesto evenly over the pizza crust, leaving a 1-inch border. Scatter the onion and bell pepper over the sauce. Distribute the cheese evenly over the top. Scatter the basil over the cheese. Arrange the shrimp in a single layer over the cheese.

5 Place the pizza in the oven on the rack or stone. (Work quickly to slide the pizza into the oven and close the door so the oven temperature doesn't drop too much.) Bake the pizza until the crust is crisp and a deep golden brown and the shrimp are pink and slightly curled, 10 to 12 minutes. Slice the pizza into wedges and serve immediately.

"Roasted Red Pepper Pesto" on page 139 ➡

QUICK AND KID-FRIENDLY PIZZA

Roasted Red Pepper Pesto

1 LARGE CLOVE GARLIC

½ TEASPOON KOSHER SALT

1 JAR (*16 OUNCES*) ROASTED RED PEPPERS, DRAINED AND BLOTTED DRY WITH PAPER TOWELS

3 TABLESPOONS FRESHLY GRATED PARMESAN CHEESE

4 LARGE FRESH BASIL LEAVES, TORN INTO LARGE PIECES

1 TABLESPOON EXTRA-VIRGIN OLIVE OIL

¾ TEASPOON SUGAR

¼ TEASPOON RED PEPPER FLAKES

MAKES 1 CUP

In a food processor fitted with the metal blade, process the garlic and salt until minced. Add the roasted red peppers, Parmesan, basil, olive oil, sugar, and red pepper flakes and process until smooth. Use immediately or transfer to a covered container and refrigerate for up to 1 week.

CHAPTER

8

Dessert Pizza

This chapter is, perhaps, icing on the cake, but we couldn't resist including a selection of dessert pizzas as a fun way to complete the book and offer a new twist to the concept of pizza. We've thrown tradition to the wind and developed a sweetly spiced dessert pizza dough that will rise up and be crisp-crackly delicious when baked. Our pizza toppings are exquisitely varied and seasonally exciting—berries for a Fourth of July bash, peaches for a late-summer backyard party, crisp apples for autumn entertaining, and the first-of-spring strawberries for a chocolate-drizzled Valentine's Day pizza affair.

Although we usually think of pizza at its best fresh and crisp, bubbling and oozing and hot from the oven, dessert pizzas are different. Tony has created a technique that keeps these pizzas crisp and divine even though the crusts are baked ahead of time—and that's terrific for entertaining. By rolling and topping the dough with just enough mozzarella cheese to keep the dough from puffing in the middle but not enough to influence the flavor, the crust can be prebaked and left at room temperature for a few hours. Right before serving, the premade toppings are added, and the pizza is ready to be cut into wedges and served. Two of the pizzas in this chapter, the Apple Strudel Pizza (page 149) and the Cranberry-Apple Pizza (page 156) benefit from a quick reheating before being served—think, warm apple pie. If you keep the oven hot, then while you're making coffee and clearing the dinner dishes, the pizza can be popped back in the oven to warm through. As with many of these pizzas, a scoop of ice cream on the side is a great accompaniment.

If you'd rather be a baker than a pizza-dough maker, you can buy fresh or frozen pizza dough and adapt the recipes. Here's the trick: Instead of rolling the dough out with flour, dust your work surface with granulated sugar that has been mixed with a little ground cinnamon and nutmeg (as if you were making cinnamon-sugar toast). Roll the dough, flipping it once to lightly coat both sides with the sugar mixture. Add the toppings and proceed with the baking directions as written. The crust won't be quite as flavorful, but it will be sweet and crisp.

Here's to sweet pizzas!

Dessert Pizza Dough

MAKES 44 OUNCES DOUGH,
ENOUGH FOR TWO 14-INCH
DESSERT PIZZAS

1 PACKAGE *(2¼ TEASPOONS)*
ACTIVE DRY YEAST

1 CUP LUKEWARM WATER
(90° TO 100°F)

1 CUP ICE-COLD WATER

1 TABLESPOON SUGAR

1 TABLESPOON TABLE SALT OR
1½ TABLESPOONS KOSHER SALT

2 TABLESPOONS OLIVE OIL

2 TABLESPOONS HONEY

5¼ TO 5½ CUPS UNBLEACHED
BREAD FLOUR, PLUS MORE FOR
DUSTING

1 TABLESPOON GROUND
CINNAMON

½ TABLESPOON FRESHLY
GROUND NUTMEG

With the addition of honey, cinnamon, and nutmeg, this pizza dough bakes up to give not only crunch to our dessert pizzas, but a rich, sweet spice flavor as well. Although this pizza recipe could be cut in half to make just one pizza crust, we envision serving a dessert pizza at a party, when there's a big group of guests. As with the other dough recipes in the book, our slow-rise method is perfect for do-ahead entertaining. Remember to make the dough at least 10 hours or the day before you plan to make pizzas.

1   In a small bowl, using a fork, stir the yeast into the lukewarm water. Set aside until the yeast dissolves, about 5 minutes.

2   In another small bowl, combine the cold water, sugar, salt, oil, and honey. Stir to dissolve the sugar and salt.

3   To make the dough by hand: Place 5¼ cups of the flour in a large bowl. Add the cinnamon and nutmeg and stir to combine. Make a well in the center of the flour and stir in the yeast mixture along with the cold water mixture. Using a wooden spoon, mix the dough, incorporating as much of the flour as possible. Turn the dough out on a lightly floured work surface and knead until soft and elastic, 10 to 12 minutes. It will still be a little sticky but shouldn't stick to your hands. Add only a minimum amount of flour to the work surface to keep the dough from sticking.

To make the dough using a mixer: Fit a heavy-duty stand mixer with the dough hook attachment. Place 5¼ cups of the flour in the mixer bowl. Add the cinnamon and nutmeg and mix on low speed

to combine. Add the yeast mixture along with the cold water mixture and mix on low speed until the flour is incorporated and the dough gathers together to form a coarse ball, about 4 minutes. Let rest for 2 minutes and then mix on medium-low speed until the dough is smooth and not sticky, about 6 minutes longer. (If the dough begins to climb up the dough hook toward the motor drive, stop the mixer and push it down. If the machine labors and the motor feels hot, stop and wait a few minutes for the motor to cool down.) Turn the dough out on a well-floured work surface and knead for 1 or 2 minutes until it forms a smooth ball, adding up to ¼ cup of additional flour, if necessary.

4   Cut the dough in half to form two even portions, each 22 ounces. With floured hands, pick up one portion of dough and pull the opposite edges together, wrapping them underneath toward the center to form a tight smooth ball. Pinch to seal. Repeat with the second portion. Place each portion in a 1-gallon lock-top plastic bag. Squeeze out all the air and seal the bags, allowing enough room for the dough to double in size. Refrigerate for at least 10 hours or up to 2 days. Remove from the refrigerator 1 hour before using to allow the dough to come to room temperature. Proceed with any dessert pizza recipe.

July 4th Triple-Berry Pizza

MAKES ONE 14-INCH PIZZA;
SERVES 8

Hooray for the red, white, and blue. What could be more fun than serving an all-American favorite—pizza—on the Fourth of July? Along with the burgers, hot dogs, corn, and coleslaw, why not finish the meal with a dessert pizza? Over a crisp and crunchy bake-ahead crust, sweet mascarpone cheese (Italian cream cheese) is spread and then covered with a cascade of fabulous summer berries. We suggest blueberries, raspberries, and strawberries, but pick and choose depending on what's freshest at the market. A light shower of lemon zest fuses the flavors, and a dusting of powdered sugar makes it all sweet and pretty.

VEGETABLE-OIL COOKING SPRAY

1 PORTION *(22 OUNCES)* DESSERT PIZZA DOUGH *(PAGE 142)*, AT ROOM TEMPERATURE

UNBLEACHED BREAD FLOUR FOR DUSTING

½ CUP *(2 OUNCES)* COARSELY SHREDDED WHOLE-MILK OR PART-SKIM, LOW-MOISTURE MOZZARELLA CHEESE

1 CUP *(8 OUNCES)* MASCARPONE CHEESE, AT ROOM TEMPERATURE

1 CUP *(½ PINT)* FRESH RASPBERRIES

1 CUP *(½ PINT)* FRESH BLUEBERRIES

8 LARGE STRAWBERRIES, HULLED AND THINLY SLICED

GRATED ZEST OF 1 LEMON

2 TO 3 TABLESPOONS POWDERED SUGAR

1   Position an oven rack on the second-lowest level in the oven and place a baking stone on the rack. Position another rack in the upper third of the oven. Preheat the oven to 500°F.

2   Coat a 14-inch pizza screen or perforated pizza pan with the cooking spray. Remove the dough from the plastic bag and place on a lightly floured work surface. Lightly dust the dough with flour. Using a rolling pin, roll the dough into a 10-inch round without rolling over the edges. Lift the dough and check to make sure the dough isn't sticking to the work surface. Shake the excess flour from the dough. Following the Dough-Tossing Techniques on page 22, toss the dough until it is stretched to a 14-inch circle and place it on the prepared pizza screen or pan. Alternatively, lay the dough on the prepared screen or pan and gently stretch the dough into a 14-inch round. Scatter the mozzarella over the dough, leaving a 1-inch border.

3   Place the pizza in the oven on the upper rack. (Work quickly to slide the pizza into the oven and close the door so the oven temperature doesn't drop too much.) Bake the pizza until the crust is crisp and a deep golden brown and the cheese is golden, 10 to 12 minutes. Using a pizza peel, lift the pizza off the screen or pan and place the crust directly on the baking stone. Using the peel or wearing thick oven mitts, remove the screen or pan from the oven. Bake the pizza until the bottom of the crust is golden brown, 2 to 3 minutes longer. Using the peel, remove the pizza from the oven and transfer to a wire rack to cool slightly. (Cool the pizza at room temperature for 5 minutes or up to 2 hours before adding the toppings.)

4   To top the pizza: Spread the mascarpone in a thin even layer over the pizza crust, leaving a 1-inch border. Scatter the berries artfully over the cheese and then sprinkle the lemon zest evenly over the berries. Using a fine-mesh sieve, dust the top of the pizza, including the crust, with powdered sugar. Slice the pizza into wedges and serve immediately.

Twistin' in the Tropics Fruit Pizza

MAKES ONE 14-INCH PIZZA;
SERVES 8

One day in 1995, Tony and *Saturday Night Live* comedian Rob Schneider were both appearing on *Mornings on 2,* a Bay Area morning news show. Tony was setting up to do a cooking segment showing the viewers how to make a fruit pizza. In walked Rob, looking worse for a night's wear and asking if there was anything to eat. He eyed the finished fruit pizza and, before Tony could say anything, picked up a slice and ate it. Giving a thumbs-up to Tony, Rob grabbed another piece. For cooking segments, the chef usually has the components ready to make a dish and a finished dish called "the hero" ready to show. By the time Tony's segment aired, Rob had eaten half of the "hero" pizza. It's that good. Do save some for your guests.

VEGETABLE-OIL COOKING SPRAY

1 PORTION *(22 OUNCES)* DESSERT PIZZA DOUGH *(PAGE 142),* AT ROOM TEMPERATURE

UNBLEACHED BREAD FLOUR FOR DUSTING

½ CUP *(2 OUNCES)* COARSELY SHREDDED WHOLE-MILK OR PART-SKIM, LOW-MOISTURE MOZZARELLA CHEESE

2 CONTAINERS *(6 OUNCES EACH)* YOPLAIT ORIGINAL LEMON BURST YOGURT, AT ROOM TEMPERATURE

8 LARGE STRAWBERRIES, HULLED AND THINLY SLICED

1   Position an oven rack on the second-lowest level in the oven and place a baking stone on the rack. Position another rack in the upper third of the oven. Preheat the oven to 500°F.

2   Coat a 14-inch pizza screen or perforated pizza pan with the cooking spray. Remove the dough from the plastic bag and place on a lightly floured work surface. Lightly dust the dough with flour. Using a rolling pin, roll the dough into a 10-inch round without rolling over the edges. Lift the dough and check to make sure the dough isn't sticking to the work surface. Shake the excess flour from the dough. Following the Dough-Tossing Techniques on page 22, toss the dough until it is stretched to a 14-inch circle and place it on the prepared pizza screen or pan. Alternatively, lay the dough on the prepared screen or pan and gently stretch the dough into a 14-inch round. Scatter the mozzarella over the dough, leaving a 1-inch border.

2 KIWIS, PEELED AND THINLY
SLICED

1 LARGE BANANA, THINLY SLICED

2 TABLESPOONS HONEY

2 TO 3 TABLESPOONS POWDERED
SUGAR

3   Place the pizza in the oven on the upper rack. (Work quickly to slide the pizza into the oven and close the door so the oven temperature doesn't drop too much.) Bake the pizza until the crust is crisp and a deep golden brown and the cheese is golden, 10 to 12 minutes. Using a pizza peel, lift the pizza off the screen or pan and place the crust directly on the baking stone. Using the peel or wearing thick oven mitts, remove the screen or pan from the oven. Bake the pizza until the bottom of the crust is golden brown, 2 to 3 minutes longer. Using the peel, remove the pizza from the oven and transfer to a wire rack to cool slightly. (Cool the pizza at room temperature for 5 minutes or up to 2 hours before adding the toppings.)

4   To top the pizza: Spread the yogurt in a thin even layer over the pizza crust, leaving a 1-inch border. Scatter the fruit artfully over the yogurt and then evenly drizzle the honey over the fruit. Using a fine-mesh sieve, dust the top of the pizza, including the crust, with powdered sugar. Slice the pizza into wedges and serve immediately.

Apple Strudel Pizza

MAKES ONE 14-INCH PIZZA;
SERVES 8

½ CUP COARSELY CHOPPED
WALNUTS

4 TABLESPOONS (½ STICK)
UNSALTED BUTTER

4 LARGE GOLDEN DELICIOUS
APPLES, PEELED, CORED, AND CUT
INTO THIN WEDGES

¼ CUP LIGHTLY PACKED BROWN
SUGAR

1 TEASPOON GROUND
CINNAMON

½ TEASPOON FRESHLY GRATED
NUTMEG

PINCH OF SALT

½ CUP RAISINS

VEGETABLE-OIL COOKING SPRAY

Diane's friend Roxane Richards Huang taught her to make real apple strudel, making and stretching the delicate dough just like Roxane's grandmother taught her to do. Not only was the dough light and buttery, but the filling was perfection with tender and caramelized apple slices, plump raisins, and crunchy toasted nuts. While developing dessert pizzas, Diane thought this filling would make a great topping for pizza. Make this pizza in the fall when the new season's crop of apples is in the market. Did we mention how good the leftovers are for breakfast?

1   Position an oven rack on the second-lowest level in the oven and place a baking stone on the rack. Position another rack in the upper third of the oven. Preheat the oven to 500°F.

2   While the oven is heating, make the apple topping: Place the nuts in a single layer on a rimmed baking sheet. Bake the nuts until lightly browned, 5 to 8 minutes, depending on how hot the oven is. (Watch the nuts carefully; they can go from toasty brown to burned in a minute's time.) Set aside to cool.

3   In a large sauté pan over medium-high heat, melt the butter and swirl to coat the pan. Add the apples and sauté, stirring constantly, until well coated with butter but still crisp, 3 minutes. Add the brown sugar, cinnamon, nutmeg, salt, and raisins. Sauté, stirring frequently, until the apples are tender but still hold their shape and the liquid is reduced, about 5 minutes. Remove from the heat and set aside. (The apple topping can be made up

to 8 hours ahead. Set aside at room temperature until ready to use. Add the walnuts just before topping the pizza.)

4   Coat a 14-inch pizza screen or perforated pizza pan with the cooking spray. Remove the dough from the plastic bag and place on a lightly floured work surface. Lightly dust the dough with flour. Using a rolling pin, roll the dough into a 10-inch round without rolling over the edges. Lift the dough and check to make sure the dough isn't sticking to the work surface. Shake the excess flour from the dough. Following the Dough-Tossing Techniques on page 22, toss the dough until it is stretched to a 14-inch circle and place it on the prepared pizza screen or pan. Alternatively, lay the dough on the prepared screen or pan and gently stretch the dough into a 14-inch round. Scatter the mozzarella over the dough, leaving a 1-inch border.

continued on next page →

1 PORTION *(22 OUNCES)* DESSERT PIZZA DOUGH *(PAGE 142)*, AT ROOM TEMPERATURE

UNBLEACHED BREAD FLOUR FOR DUSTING

½ CUP *(2 OUNCES)* COARSELY SHREDDED WHOLE-MILK OR PART-SKIM, LOW-MOISTURE MOZZARELLA CHEESE

2 TO 3 TABLESPOONS POWDERED SUGAR

1 PINT VANILLA ICE CREAM

5   Place the pizza in the oven on the upper rack. (Work quickly to slide the pizza into the oven and close the door so the oven temperature doesn't drop too much.) Bake the pizza until the crust is crisp and golden brown and the cheese is golden, 9 minutes. Using a pizza peel, lift the pizza off the screen or pan and place the crust directly on the baking stone. Using the peel or wearing thick oven mitts, remove the screen or pan from the oven. Bake the pizza until the bottom of the crust is golden brown, 2 minutes longer. Using the peel, remove the pizza from the oven and transfer to a wire rack to cool slightly. (Cool the pizza at room temperature for 5 minutes or up to 2 hours before adding the toppings.)

6   To top and finish baking the pizza: Have the oven at 500°F. Stir the toasted walnuts into the apple mixture. Slide the pizza crust onto the pizza peel. Spread the apple mixture in an even layer over the pizza crust, leaving a 1-inch border. Slide the pizza crust directly onto the baking stone and bake the pizza until the apple mixture is heated through, about 5 minutes. Using the pizza peel, transfer the pizza to a cutting board. Using a fine-mesh sieve, dust the top of the pizza, including the crust, with powdered sugar. Slice the pizza into wedges and serve with scoops of vanilla ice cream.

Sweetheart Pizza with Chocolate and Strawberries

MAKES ONE 14-INCH HEART-
SHAPED PIZZA; SERVES 6

½ CUP (4 OUNCES) MASCARPONE
CHEESE, AT ROOM TEMPERATURE

2 CUPS (12 OUNCES) WHOLE-MILK
RICOTTA CHEESE

1 CUP POWDERED SUGAR, PLUS
MORE FOR DUSTING

1½ TEASPOONS PURE VANILLA
EXTRACT

½ CUP MINIATURE SEMISWEET
CHOCOLATE CHIPS

VEGETABLE-OIL COOKING SPRAY

1 PORTION (22 OUNCES) DESSERT
PIZZA DOUGH (PAGE 142), AT
ROOM TEMPERATURE

Valentine's Day at Pyzano's is always fun, because Tony makes a heart-shaped dessert pizza as a special. Over a prebaked pizza crust Tony spreads a sweetened ricotta mixture that has been dotted with mini chocolate chips. Halved strawberries are artfully arranged over the top, dusted with powdered sugar, and then drizzled with a lusty and rich, deep-dark chocolate sauce. It's irresistible—a lovers' delight. For fun, buy an extra-large heart-shaped cookie cutter and make individual sweetheart pizzas.

1   Position an oven rack on the second-lowest level in the oven and place a baking stone on the rack. Position another rack in the upper third of the oven. Preheat the oven to 500°F.

2   While the oven is heating, make the topping: In a mixing bowl, combine the mascarpone, ricotta, 1 cup powdered sugar, and vanilla until all the sugar is incorporated. Gently fold in the chocolate chips. Set aside. (The ricotta topping can be made up to 1 day in advance. Bring to room temperature before topping the pizza.)

3   Coat a 14-inch pizza screen or perforated pizza pan with the cooking spray. Remove the dough from the plastic bag and place on a lightly floured work surface. Lightly dust the dough with flour. Using a rolling pin, roll the dough into a 10-inch round without rolling over the edges. Lift the dough and check to make sure the dough isn't sticking to the work surface. Shake the excess flour from the dough. Following the Dough-Tossing Techniques on page 22, toss the dough until it is stretched to a 14-inch circle and place it on the prepared pizza screen or pan. Alternatively, keeping the dough on the work surface, gently stretch the dough into a 14-inch round. Using a pizza cutter, free-form cut the dough into a heart shape that is 14 inches across at the widest point. If you have a heart-shaped cake pan, use that as a template, or make a template using parchment paper. Carefully transfer the dough to the prepared screen or pan. Scatter the mozzarella over the dough, leaving a 1-inch border.

continued on next page →

UNBLEACHED BREAD FLOUR FOR
DUSTING

½ CUP *(2 OUNCES)* COARSELY
SHREDDED WHOLE-MILK OR
PART-SKIM, LOW-MOISTURE
MOZZARELLA CHEESE

1 PINT STRAWBERRIES, STEMMED
AND HALVED LENGTHWISE

2 TO 3 TABLESPOONS GOOD-
QUALITY STORE-BOUGHT DARK
CHOCOLATE SAUCE OR HOT
FUDGE SAUCE, WARMED

4   Place the pizza in the oven on the upper rack. (Work quickly to slide the pizza into the oven and close the door so the oven temperature doesn't drop too much.) Bake the pizza until the crust is crisp and a deep golden brown and the cheese is golden, 10 to 12 minutes. Using a pizza peel, lift the pizza off the screen or pan and place the crust directly on the baking stone. Using the peel or wearing thick oven mitts, remove the screen or pan from the oven. Bake the pizza until the bottom of the crust is golden brown, 2 to 3 minutes longer. Using the peel, remove the pizza from the oven and transfer to a wire rack to cool slightly. (Cool the pizza at room temperature for 5 minutes or up to 2 hours before adding the toppings.)

5   To top the pizza: Spread the ricotta mixture in a thin even layer over the pizza crust, leaving a 1-inch border. Arrange the strawberries artfully over top. Using a fine-mesh sieve, dust the top of the pizza, including the crust, with powdered sugar. Drizzle the chocolate sauce over top. Slice the pizza into wedges and serve immediately.

Cannoli Pizza

MAKES ONE 14-INCH PIZZA;
SERVES 8

Tony loves cannoli, the wonderful Italian dessert consisting of a deep-fried tubular-shaped pastry shell filled with a sweetened ricotta cheese, usually mixed with bits of chocolate and/or candied fruit. He grew up eating them, and thought when his wedding day came those little cannoli would be the perfect dessert to serve along with the wedding cake. Tony and his then bride-to-be, Julie, went to North Beach in San Francisco in search of the best cannoli. Having sampled at least a dozen different cannoli, they found their favorite and ordered 150 for the reception. While sampling, it occurred to Tony that the filling would make a great topping for a dessert pizza. This pizza is a delectable Italian treat.

¾ CUP *(6 OUNCES)* MASCARPONE CHEESE, AT ROOM TEMPERATURE

3 CUPS *(18 OUNCES)* WHOLE-MILK RICOTTA CHEESE

1½ CUPS POWDERED SUGAR, PLUS MORE FOR DUSTING

¼ CUP CANDIED OR GLACÉ LEMON PEEL, CUT INTO ¼-INCH DICE

½ CUP CANDIED OR GLACÉ CHERRIES, HALVED

½ CUP MINIATURE SEMISWEET CHOCOLATE CHIPS

VEGETABLE-OIL COOKING SPRAY

1   Position an oven rack on the second-lowest level in the oven and place a baking stone on the rack. Position another rack in the upper third of the oven. Preheat the oven to 500°F.

2   While the oven is heating, make the topping: In a mixing bowl, stir together the mascarpone, ricotta, and 1½ cups powdered sugar until all the sugar is incorporated. Gently fold in the lemon peel, cherries, and chocolate chips. Set aside. (The ricotta topping can be made up to 1 day in advance. Bring to room temperature before topping the pizza.)

3   Coat a 14-inch pizza screen or perforated pizza pan with the cooking spray. Remove the dough from the plastic bag and place on a lightly floured work surface. Lightly dust the dough with flour. Using a rolling pin, roll the dough into a 10-inch round without rolling over the edges. Lift the dough and check to make sure the dough isn't sticking to the work surface. Shake the excess flour from the dough. Following the Dough-Tossing Techniques on page 22, toss the dough until it is stretched to a 14-inch circle and place it on the prepared pizza screen or pan. Alternatively, lay the dough on the prepared screen or pan and gently stretch the dough into a 14-inch round. Scatter the mozzarella over the dough, leaving a 1-inch border.

1 PORTION *(22 OUNCES)* DESSERT
PIZZA DOUGH *(PAGE 142)*, AT
ROOM TEMPERATURE

UNBLEACHED BREAD FLOUR FOR
DUSTING

½ CUP *(2 OUNCES)* COARSELY
SHREDDED WHOLE-MILK OR
PART-SKIM, LOW-MOISTURE
MOZZARELLA CHEESE

¼ CUP GOOD-QUALITY STORE-
BOUGHT DARK CHOCOLATE
SAUCE OR HOT FUDGE SAUCE,
WARMED

4   Place the pizza in the oven on the upper rack.
(Work quickly to slide the pizza into the oven and
close the door so the oven temperature doesn't
drop too much.) Bake the pizza until the crust is
crisp and a deep golden brown and the cheese
is golden, 10 to 12 minutes. Using a pizza peel,
lift the pizza off the screen or pan and place the
crust directly on the baking stone. Using the peel
or wearing thick oven mitts, remove the screen
or pan from the oven. Bake the pizza until the
bottom of the crust is golden brown, 2 to 3 minutes longer. Using the peel, remove the pizza
from the oven and transfer to a wire rack to cool
slightly. (Cool the pizza at room temperature
for 5 minutes or up to 2 hours before adding
the toppings.)

5   To top the pizza: Spread the ricotta mixture
in a thin even layer over the pizza crust, leaving a
1-inch border. Using a fine-mesh sieve, dust the
top of the pizza, including the crust, with powdered sugar. Drizzle the chocolate sauce over top.
Slice the pizza into wedges and serve immediately.

Cranberry-Apple Pizza

MAKES ONE 14-INCH PIZZA;
SERVES 8

½ CUP (*1 STICK*) UNSALTED
BUTTER

3 LARGE GOLDEN DELICIOUS
APPLES, PEELED, CORED, AND
CUT INTO ½-INCH CHUNKS

2 TABLESPOONS, PLUS ¼ CUP
LIGHTLY PACKED DARK BROWN
SUGAR

2 TABLESPOONS GRANULATED
SUGAR

½ TEASPOON GROUND
CINNAMON

2 CUPS SWEETENED DRIED
CRANBERRIES

Diane was skeptical when Tony told her about his idea for a cranberry-apple pizza. Trying to convince her Tony said, "Think of it as a fall tart with apples and cranberries, except it's a pizza. It could even be a Thanksgiving dessert." Diane no longer needs to be convinced; in fact, this is her and her family's favorite dessert pizza—they fought over the leftovers for breakfast!

Unlike some of the other dessert pizzas in this chapter that are made by first prebaking the crust, this pizza is baked as a traditional pizza, with the toppings arranged on top of the rolled out dough. That doesn't mean this need be a last-minute dessert; it can be made several hours in advance and then reheated just before serving. In addition, the filling and dough can each be made in advance.

1   Position an oven rack on the second-lowest level in the oven and place a baking stone on the rack. Position another rack in the upper third of the oven. Preheat the oven to 500°F.

2   While the oven is heating, make the apple topping: In a large sauté pan over medium-high heat, melt the butter and swirl to coat the pan. Add the apples, the 2 tablespoons brown sugar, the granulated sugar, and the cinnamon and sauté, stirring frequently, until the apples are tender but still hold their shape, about 8 minutes. Add the cranberries and continue to sauté, stirring occasionally, until the cranberries are soft and plump and the liquid is reduced, 5 to 6 minutes. Remove from the heat and set aside. (The apple topping can be made up to 8 hours ahead. Set aside at room temperature until ready to use.)

3   Coat a 14-inch pizza screen or perforated pizza pan with the cooking spray. Remove the dough from the plastic bag and place on a lightly floured work surface. Lightly dust the dough with flour. Using a rolling pin, roll the dough into a 10-inch round without rolling over the edges. Lift the dough and check to make sure the dough isn't sticking to the work surface. Shake the excess flour from the dough. Following the Dough-Tossing Techniques on page 22, toss the dough until it is stretched to a 14-inch circle and place it on the prepared pizza screen or pan. Alternatively, lay the dough on the prepared screen or pan and gently stretch the dough into a 14-inch round. Spread the apple mixture over the dough, leaving a 1-inch border. Evenly sprinkle the ¼ cup brown sugar over top, including the edges of the dough.

VEGETABLE-OIL COOKING SPRAY

1 PORTION *(22 OUNCES)* DESSERT PIZZA DOUGH *(PAGE 142)*, AT ROOM TEMPERATURE

UNBLEACHED BREAD FLOUR FOR DUSTING

2 TO 3 TABLESPOONS POWDERED SUGAR

1 PINT VANILLA ICE CREAM

4   Place the pizza in the oven on the upper rack. (Work quickly to slide the pizza into the oven and close the door so the oven temperature doesn't drop too much.) Bake the pizza until the crust is crisp and golden brown, 8 to 10 minutes. Using a pizza peel, lift the pizza off the screen or pan and place the crust directly on the baking stone. Using the peel or wearing thick oven mitts, remove the screen or pan from the oven. Bake the pizza until the bottom of the crust is golden brown, 3 to 4 minutes longer. Using the peel, remove the pizza from the oven and transfer to a cutting board. Using a fine-mesh sieve, dust the top of the pizza, including the crust, with powdered sugar. Slice the pizza into wedges and serve with scoops of vanilla ice cream.

Caramel, Ginger, and Fresh Peach Pizza

MAKES ONE 14-INCH PIZZA;
SERVES 8

Make this sweet pizza for summer entertaining, when peaches are ripe and juicy and temperatures are hot. Luscious, drippingly-sweet peaches are artfully arranged over a prebaked pizza crust that has been sprinkled with gingersnap crumbs. Warm and gooey caramel sauce is drizzled over top and the whole confection is dusted with powdered sugar. A cold blast of ice cream is downright decadent on the side.

VEGETABLE-OIL COOKING SPRAY

1 PORTION *(22 OUNCES)* DESSERT PIZZA DOUGH *(PAGE 142)*, AT ROOM TEMPERATURE

UNBLEACHED BREAD FLOUR FOR DUSTING

½ CUP *(2 OUNCES)* COARSELY SHREDDED WHOLE-MILK OR PART-SKIM, LOW-MOISTURE MOZZARELLA CHEESE

5 LARGE RIPE BUT FIRM PEACHES, PEELED, PITTED, AND CUT INTO ¼-INCH-THICK WEDGES

GRATED ZEST OF 1 LEMON

1 TABLESPOON FRESH LEMON JUICE

1   Position an oven rack on the second-lowest level in the oven and place a baking stone on the rack. Position another rack in the upper third of the oven. Preheat the oven to 500°F.

2   Coat a 14-inch pizza screen or perforated pizza pan with the cooking spray. Remove the dough from the plastic bag and place on a lightly floured work surface. Lightly dust the dough with flour. Using a rolling pin, roll the dough into a 10-inch round without rolling over the edges. Lift the dough and check to make sure the dough isn't sticking to the work surface. Shake the excess flour from the dough. Following the Dough-Tossing Techniques on page 22, toss the dough until it is stretched to a 14-inch circle and place it on the prepared pizza screen or pan. Alternatively, lay the dough on the prepared screen or pan and gently stretch the dough into a 14-inch round. Scatter the mozzarella over the dough, leaving a 1-inch border.

3   Place the pizza in the oven on the upper rack. (Work quickly to slide the pizza into the oven and close the door so the oven temperature doesn't drop too much.) Bake the pizza until the crust is crisp and golden brown and the cheese is golden, 8 minutes. Using a pizza peel, lift the pizza off the screen or pan and place the crust directly on the baking stone. Using the peel or wearing thick oven mitts, remove the screen or pan from the oven. Bake the pizza until the bottom of the crust is golden brown, 2 minutes longer. Using the peel, remove the pizza from the oven and transfer to a wire rack to cool slightly. (Cool the pizza at room temperature for 5 minutes or up to 2 hours before adding the toppings.)

7 CRISP GINGERSNAP COOKIES
(ABOUT 1½ INCHES IN DIAMETER)

¼ CUP GOOD-QUALITY STORE-
BOUGHT CARAMEL SAUCE,
WARMED

2 TO 3 TABLESPOONS POWDERED
SUGAR

1 PINT VANILLA ICE CREAM

4   While the pizza is baking, prepare the top-pings: In a bowl, toss the peaches with the lemon zest and juice. Place the cookies in a heavy lock-top plastic bag and, using a rolling pin, crush the cookies to make fine crumbs. Alternatively, crush the cookies in a food processor. Set aside.

5   To top and finish baking the pizza: Have the oven at 500°F. Slide the pizza crust onto the pizza peel. Scatter ¼ cup of the gingersnap crumbs evenly over the pizza crust, leaving a 1-inch border. Drizzle the caramel sauce over the gingersnap crumbs. Lay the peach slices in slightly overlapping concentric circles over the cookie crumbs, leaving a 1-inch border. Sprinkle the remaining cookie crumbs evenly over the peaches. Slide the pizza crust directly onto the pizza stone and bake the pizza until the crust is well browned on the bottom and the peaches are tender, hot, and glistening, about 5 minutes. Using the pizza peel, transfer the pizza to a cutting board. Using a fine-mesh sieve, dust the top of the pizza, including the crust, with powdered sugar. Slice the pizza into wedges and serve with scoops of vanilla ice cream.

Sources

BARBECUE SAUCE
(a biased favorite)

......

BRYANT'S BARBECUE SAUCE
ARTHUR BRYANT'S BARBECUE RESTAURANT
1727 BROOKLYN STREET
KANSAS CITY, MO 64127
WWW.ARTHURBRYANTSBBQ.COM

CHEESE

**AMERICAN-MADE BUFFALO'S MILK
(*bufala*) MOZZARELLA**

......

BUBALUS BUBALIS, INC.
18207 S. BROADWAY
GARDENA, CA 90248
PHONE: 310-515-0500
FAX: 310-515-5125
WWW.MOZZARELLADIBUFALA.NET

......

STAR HILL DAIRY
P.O. BOX 295
SOUTH WOODSTOCK, VT 05071
802-457-4540
WWW.WOODSTOCKWATERBUFFALO.COM

**AMERICAN-MADE ITALIAN-STYLE
COW'S MILK CHEESES**

......

BORRELLI LATTICINI
3021 W. DAKOTA AVENUE
FRESNO, CA 93722
559-226-6200
WWW.BORRELLILATTICINI.COM
*Mozzarella; fresh mozzarella; Scamorza; Caciocavallo;
provolone; ricotta*

......

CANTARE FOODS, INC.
7688 MIRAMAR ROAD
SAN DIEGO, CA 92126
858-578-8490
Fresh mozzarella; whole-milk ricotta; mascarpone

......

GIOIA CHEESE COMPANY
1605 POTRERO AVENUE
SOUTH EL MONTE, CA 91733
626-444-6015
GIOIACHEESE@HOTMAIL.COM
*Mascarpone; smoked mozzarella; ricotta; Scamorza;
Caciocavallo*

......

MOZZARELLA COMPANY
2944 ELM STREET
DALLAS, TX 75226
800-798-2954
WWW.MOZZCO.COM
*Fresh mozzarella; smoked mozzarella; smoked
Scamorza; mascarpone*

......

**TUTTO LATTE MOZZARELLA
CHEESE COMPANY**
5027 HEINTZ STREET
BALDWIN PARK, CA 91706
626-337-8154
WWW.TUTTOLATTE.COM
Fresh mozzarella; ricotta; mascarpone; Scamorza

IMPORTED ITALIAN CHEESE

......

ONLINE GOURMET PRODUCTS
877-IGOURMET
WWW.IGOURMET.COM
(Cheese from around the world)

FLOUR

CAPUTO FLOUR *(farina di grano
tenero tipo 00)*
AVAILABLE FROM
WWW.CHEFSWAREHOUSE.COM

......

KING ARTHUR FLOUR
P.O. BOX 876
NORWICH, VT 05055
800-827-6836
WWW.BAKERSCATALOGUE.COM
All-purpose flour; unbleached bread flour; rye flour, etc.

ITALIAN SPECIALTY FOODS

ITALY'S BEST FOODS
718-860-2949
WWW.GUSTIAMO.COM

PIZZA TOOLS

BEST MANUFACTURERS, INC.
WWW.BESTMFRS.COM
Peels, baking stones, cutters, screens, pizza pans

......

CLEVER GEAR
800-829-2685
WWW.CLEVERGEAR.COM
Pizza forks

......

INSTAWARES.COM
(RESTAURANT SUPPLY SUPERSTORE ONLINE)
800-892-3622
WWW.INSTAWARES.COM
*Aluminum perforated pizza screens made by American
Metalcraft; aluminum mesh screens; peels; cutters;
pizza pans*

......

KING ARTHUR FLOUR
P.O. BOX 876
NORWICH, VT 05055
800-827-6836
WWW.BAKERSCATALOGUE.COM

......

PIZZATOOLS.COM
509-468-8691
Everything for the pizza maker; an industry online source

SUR LA TABLE
800-243-0852
WWW.SURLATABLE.COM
Peels, baking stones, cutters, rocker knife, screens, pizza pans, Hearth Kit

WILLIAMS-SONOMA
877-812-6235
WWW.WILLIAMS-SONOMA.COM
Baking stones, cutters, pizza pans, screens

INSTRUCTIONAL PIZZA TOSSING DVD AND PRO DOUGH

PRO DOUGH *(synthetic, glow-in-the-dark pizza dough that looks and feels like real dough)*
PRO DOUGH USA
    "TOSS LIKE A PRO" BASIC STEPS
PRO DOUGH USA
    "TOSS LIKE A PRO" INTERMEDIATE STEPS
PRO DOUGH USA
    "TOSS LIKE A PRO" ADVANCED STEPS
800-946-8224
WWW.PRODOUGHUSA.COM
Watch and learn to throw dough from Tony Gemignani.

WOOD-FIRED OVENS

EARTHSTONE
800-840-4915
WWW.EARTHSTONEOVENS.COM
Wood-fired ovens

KIKO DENZER
541-438-4300
WWW.INTABAS.COM/KIKODENZER.HTML
Workshops to build your own wood-fired mud oven

MUGNAINI
888-887-7206
WWW.MUGNAINI.COM
Italy's original wood-fired oven

OVEN CRAFTERS
415-663-9010
WWW.OVENCRAFTERS.NET
Customized wood-fired brick ovens

WOODSTONE CORPORATION
800-988-8074
WWW.WOODSTONE-CORP.COM
Stone-hearth cooking equipment

PIZZERIAS
(a list of Diane and Tony's favorite pizzerias in the United States and Canada)

ARIZONA

PIZZERIA BIANCO
622 E. ADAMS STREET
PHOENIX, AZ 85004
602-258-8300

CALIFORNIA

A16
2355 CHESTNUT STREET
SAN FRANCISCO, CA 94123
415-771-2216

ANTICA PIZZERIA
VILLA MARINA MARKETPLACE
13455 MAXELLA AVENUE
MARINA DEL REY, CA 90292
310-577-8182

GINA'S PIZZA AND PASTERIA
420 IRIS AVENUE
CORONA DEL MAR, CA 92625
949-673-1121

PIZZA MY HEART/PIZZA A-GO-GO
220 UNIVERSITY AVENUE
PALO ALTO, CA 94301
650-327-9500

PIZZETTA 211
211 23RD AVENUE
SAN FRANCISCO, CA 94116
415-379-9880

PYZANO'S PIZZERIA
3835 E. CASTRO VALLEY BOULEVARD
580 MARKET PLACE
CASTRO VALLEY, CA 94552
510-881-8878

TOMMASO RISTORANTE ITALIANO
1042 KEARNY STREET
SAN FRANCISCO, CA 94133
415-398-9696

ZACHERY'S CHICAGO PIZZA
5801 COLLEGE AVENUE
BERKELEY, CA 94705
510-655-6385

COLORADO

CUCINA COLORE
3041 E. 3RD AVENUE
DENVER, CO 80206
303-393-6917

CONNECTICUT

FRANK PEPE PIZZERIA NAPOLETANA
157 WOOSTER STREET (LITTLE ITALY)
NEW HAVEN, CT 06511
203-865-5762

ILLINOIS

EDWARDO'S PIZZA
1321 E. 57TH STREET
CHICAGO, IL 60637
312-241-7960

......
GINO'S EAST
633 N. WELLS STREET
CHICAGO, IL 60610
312-943-1124

......
GIORDANO'S
730 N. RUSH STREET
CHICAGO, IL 60611
312-951-0747

......
LOU MALNATI
439 N. WELLS STREET
CHICAGO, IL 60610
312-828-9800

......
NANCY'S
2930 N. BROADWAY
CHICAGO, IL 60657
773-883-1977

......
PIZZERIA UNO
29 E. OHIO STREET
CHICAGO, IL 60611
312-321-1000

LOUISIANA

......
DEANGELO'S
7955 BLUEBONNET BOULEVARD
BATON ROUGE, LA 70810
225-761-4465

MINNESOTA

......
GREEN MILL RESTAURANT
57 HAMLINE AVENUE SOUTH
ST. PAUL, MN 55105
651-698-0353

NEW YORK
......
BROTHER'S PIZZERIA
730 PORT RICHMOND AVENUE
STATEN ISLAND, NY 10302
718-442-2332

......
JOHN'S PIZZA
278 BLEECKER STREET
NEW YORK, NY 10014
212-243-1680

......
GOODFELLA'S RESTAURANT & BAR
9602 3RD AVENUE
BROOKLYN, NY 11209
718-833-6200

......
GRIMALDI'S PIZZERIA
19 OLD FULTON STREET
BROOKLYN, NY 11201
718-858-4300

......
LOMBARDI'S
32 SPRING STREET
NEW YORK, NY 10012
212-941-7994

......
PATSY'S PIZZA
2287-91 FIRST AVENUE
NEW YORK, NY 10035
212-534-9783

......
RAY'S PIZZA
27 PRINCE STREET
NEW YORK, NY 10012
212-966-1960

......
SALVATORE'S COAL OVEN PIZZA
124 SHORE ROAD
PORT WASHINGTON, NY 11050
516-883-8457

......
TOTONNO'S PIZZERIA NAPOLITANO
1524 NEPTUNE AVENUE
BROOKLYN, NY 11224
718-372-8606

PENNSYLVANIA

......
ROBERTO'S PIZZERIA
BELLEVUE LOCATION (JUST OUTSIDE
   PITTSBURGH)
516 LINCOLN AVENUE
BELLEVUE, PA 15202
412-761-1077
WWW.ROBERTOSPIZZERIA.COM

RHODE ISLAND

......
AL FORNO RESTAURANT
577 S. MAIN STREET
PROVIDENCE, RI 02903
401-273-9760

TEXAS

......
ARCODORO & POMODORO
2708 ROUTH STREET
DALLAS, TX 75201
214-871-1924
POMODORO@ARCODORO.COM

CANADA

......
**(DINO CICCONE'S) WORLD FAMOUS
   EASTOWN BISTRO**
189 FAIRHAVEN CIRCLE
LONDON, ONTARIO N5W 1E3

Index

Table of equivalents

The exact equivalents in the following tables have been rounded for convenience.

LIQUID/DRY MEASURES

U.S.	METRIC
¼ TEASPOON	1.25 MILLILITERS
½ TEASPOON	2.5 MILLILITERS
1 TEASPOON	5 MILLILITERS
1 TABLESPOON (3 TEASPOONS)	15 MILLILITERS
1 FLUID OUNCE (2 TABLESPOONS)	30 MILLILITERS
¼ CUP	60 MILLILITERS
⅓ CUP	80 MILLILITERS
½ CUP	120 MILLILITERS
1 CUP	240 MILLILITERS
1 PINT (2 CUPS)	480 MILLILITERS
1 QUART (4 CUPS, 32 OUNCES)	960 MILLILITERS
1 GALLON (4 QUARTS)	3.84 LITERS
1 OUNCE (BY WEIGHT)	28 GRAMS
1 POUND	454 GRAMS
2.2 POUNDS	1 KILOGRAM

LENGTH

U.S.	METRIC
⅛ INCH	3 MILLIMETERS
¼ INCH	6 MILLIMETERS
½ INCH	12 MILLIMETERS
1 INCH	2.5 CENTIMETERS

OVEN TEMPERATURE

FAHRENHEIT	CELSIUS	GAS
250	120	½
275	140	1
300	150	2
325	160	3
350	180	4
375	190	5
400	200	6
425	220	7
450	230	8
475	240	9
500	260	10